HOW TO MEET A LOVELY ASIAN GIRL
... AND BRING HER HOME!

Keith Connes

Cover design by Dale Ziemianski

Butterfield Press
283 Carlo Drive
Goleta, CA 93117
805-964-8627
info@butterfieldpress.com
http://Men4AsianWomen.com

Contents

INTRODUCTION

Ever fantasize about traveling to an Asian country and bringing a charming young woman home to live with you? Take heart – that fantasy is very much within your grasp! It happens all the time. In fact, I have done it *three* times!

You can start your shopping from the comfort of your home and see what's available for as little as $25. Of course, if you like what you see, be prepared to put out a significant amount of time and money, but it will be well worth the investment if your life becomes filled with new-found happiness – as mine has!

There are other books on meeting Asian women and some of them provide good information. However, my book goes further than others. First of all, I reveal my personal experiences gained from a total of 21 trips to Thailand and the Philippines. So you'll get a realistic idea of what you can expect when you go girl-hunting in foreign lands.

Equally important, I will educate you on the tricky immigration procedures necessary to get your lady to the US. Many people are under the impression that an American citizen can marry a foreigner in her country and bring her right home. Not true. You must apply for a visa for her and there is a waiting period usually of three to ten months (or more, if there are mistakes in the application) before the application is approved. *If* it is approved. Many applications are rejected, sometimes for reasons that seem frivolous.

For example, how many photos of the two of you should you provide to prove to the Immigration Service that your relationship is sincere? The surprising answer doesn't appear on any official document, but the pros know what the bureaucrats really want and I'll reveal that information to you.

Here's a question about a decision that can make a big difference in the cost of bringing your girl home: Is it worthwhile to hire someone to prepare and file her visa application, and what are the practical differences between hiring a licensed immigration attorney and a less-expensive paralegal? I've used both types, and I'll tell you who they are and how much they charge.

This book will give you much more information than I've seen elsewhere regarding the immigration process – what it can cost, how much time it can take, what to do and what *not* to do in dealing with the various layers of bureaucracy, and the techniques that will help your lady get through the crucial interview at the US Embassy in her country. One important tip: If at all possible, *be there with her*.

Both the spousal visa and the fiancée visa have their respective advantages and drawbacks, and I'll explain those in detail. (Forget about other types of visa, such as the tourist visa, which is practically impossible to obtain and can cause you serious problems if you apply later for the spousal or fiancée visa.)

Also, if you are thinking of moving to your future wife's country, this book will provide you with insights on the legalities, benefits, and possible drawbacks you will face.

Here's an important cultural question: In which country does religion dictate governmental law and how could that affect your love life? I'll explain in detail and I'll provide a lot more information on significant cultural differences between East and West.

I am not going to paint the rosy picture I've seen in other books. Instead, I am going to provide a candid description of the pleasures – and pitfalls – of venturing overseas to find the girl of your dreams. I will focus on Thailand and the Philippines because I have had most of my personal experiences in those countries. However, much of the information in this book applies to other countries as well.

If you're not sure about getting married but would like to do some sampling and enjoy the intimate companionship of charming, respectable Thai and/or Philippine women (*not prostitutes*), see my chapter titled "Sex without Marriage." I will share my own adventures, during which I enjoyed the companionship of an assortment of delightful girlfriends. I will also describe in mortifying detail my foolhardy mistakes to help you avoid doing the same.

For me, it has been an extraordinary adventure, and despite some setbacks, one that has been most exciting and rewarding. I am confident that when you finish this book you will have new insights and valuable information that will help you on your own journey of meeting wonderful women and finding the companion of your dreams.

1

WHY CHOOSE AN ASIAN GIRL?

It's easy to see why many American men are attracted to Asian women: Long black hair, large eyes, a pert nose, and often a slender graceful shape. But more important than the appearance of these girls is their culture that teaches them to respect and take care of their man. This can be a delightful surprise to those of us who feel that a lot of American women are just plain spoiled. And perhaps most important for the older man who seeks a young wife is the fact that a large age gap is readily accepted in countries such as Thailand and the Philippines.

Actually, a lot of Asian girls *prefer* an older American man to a young man from their own country. That's because they don't have a high opinion of the local lads, many of whom smoke too much, drink too much, gamble too much, and chase other women. As a result of these tendencies many girls seek a mature American, regardless of age – a caring, faithful, and responsible husband who can provide them with a decent standard of living. I have often been asked by lovely young Thai girls and Filipinas if I know of any single Americans that I could send their way. I hope to do it through this book.

When you visit either Thailand or the Philippines, you'll see many mixed couples. The guy might be in his 30s or 40s, but quite often he's in his 50s, 60s, or even older. Hanging onto his arm is his wife in her 20s or 30s, sometimes with their kids clustered around.

Want an extreme example of an age difference? I am married to a lovely Filipina. At this writing, she is 25 years old and I am 87. We have been married for three years, we are bonded together like Krazy Glue, and we are totally happy. I should add that I am not wealthy nor am I a charismatic silver fox type, but I have a clean lifestyle and my top priority is to take good care of my dear wife.

As the saying goes, if I can do it, so can you. There are thousands of desirable Asian girls out there right now, many of them on Internet websites, waiting eagerly for you. You'll find many who are sincere and honest, and will make great lifetime companions. Others know how to play the part but are actually out to take you for all they can get. I can't promise you a foolproof way of distinguishing the bad apples from the good, but in the chapters that follow I'll give you helpful clues – some of which I've picked up the hard way and others that I've heard about from other wife-seekers.

By the way, I guess this is as good a place as any to try to deflect hate mail from those devotees of political correctness who resent any reference to a female of 18-plus years as a "girl." I use the word frequently, preferring it to the rather formal "young woman," (many of whom casually refer to themselves as "girls" or even "guys").

In the next chapter I'll describe some East-West cultural differences you'll need to be aware of.

2

WHAT ABOUT CULTURAL DIFFERENCES?

There's a famous poem that begins, "Oh, East is East and West is West and never the twain shall meet." This might have been true when Rudyard Kipling penned those words, but it does not apply today. The United States in particular, through its vast output of movies, TV programs – and now the Internet – has exported its culture of entertainment, fashions, and behavior worldwide.

McDonalds, KFC, and Shakeys have impacted Asian tastes, for better or worse. English is widely spoken, particularly by the younger people. (Basic English is taught to Philippine school children, starting in kindergarten.)

So you should not have much trouble finding a Filipina or Thai girl whom you'd be as comfortable with as the girl next door. However, it's best to be aware of some cultural differences you're likely to encounter.

Family Togetherness

Perhaps as much because of economics as cultural tradition, Asians tend to place a lot of emphasis on family togetherness, often at the expense of individual independence. Whereas in our culture, when children reach adulthood and usually move into a place of their own, Asian offspring typically remain at home even after they marry and produce their own kids. So it is normal to have several generations happily and noisily co-existing under the same roof. (It certainly solves the baby-sitter problem!) When the parents get old they are not sent off to a senior living facility but continue to take part in family life.

Most Thai girls and Filipinas have a strong sense of indebtedness to their parents for having conceived and raised them. Not surprisingly, the parents encourage this burden of indebtedness, which can last a lifetime – but oddly enough, this applies mostly to the girls.

The boys are raised as princes. Some of them might actually get a job while others are quite content to sit around and smoke, drink beer, and chase girls. When they marry, sometimes jilting one or two fiancées along the way, many of them consider it a sign of prestige if they can afford to maintain a mistress in a separate household, perhaps fathering a second set of children.

When you marry one of their daughters it is generally accepted that you will take her to your own country, although if that is your intention you need to make it clear at the outset. On the other hand, you might find it desirable to move to her country and set up your own household there.

Either way, your wife will continue to feel responsible for the well-being of her family members and will often want to provide ongoing financial support. If you are unable or unwilling to give that support, your wife will probably want to work and send part or all of her earnings to her family. It is best to have a clear understanding with your future wife about any such financial expectations, especially if you plan to raise a family of your own.

By the way, "American" and "rich" are thought to be synonymous and your protestations to the contrary are likely to fall on deaf ears, at least at the beginning. I am not suggesting that you refuse to offer any financial assistance to the family, but be prepared to discover that the more you provide, the more will likely be expected. Your most effective defense is probably the word "No," repeated as firmly and as often as necessary.

The Dowry

Here is one significant cultural difference between Thailand and the Philippines: Thailand has a dowry system and the Philippines does not. This delightful custom requires a man (Thai or foreigner) who wants to marry a Thai girl to give a cash payment to her parents prior to the wedding.

The dowries typically range from 100,000 to 300,000 baht – roughly $3,300 to $10,000 – but they could be higher or lower. (Farm girls come cheaper than girls from well-to-do families.) Many Thai parents whose children are still living with them will not let you take their daughter on a "get acquainted" trip, i.e., to a hotel, until there is an engagement party. An important feature of the engagement party is a down payment on the dowry – anywhere from 10 to 30 percent.

If there is a traditional wedding ceremony, the cash for the entire dowry is on display, so the wedding guests can see how much the bride is worth. Sometimes the groom can't afford a large enough dowry. To keep the family from losing face, he somehow scrapes together the requisite amount, and after the ceremony, part of it is quietly returned to him.

Does all this sound as if you're buying your wife? In a word, yes. Although you might find exceptions, it goes with the territory, if that territory is Thailand.

Lending Money

If you lend money to a Filipino – especially a family member of your girlfriend or wife – don't expect to get it back. You might be given a very specific promise of repayment – for example, at the end of the month when the borrower will be paid for some work – but whatever the story, just forget it.

If, after having waited for some time, you bring up the subject of the loan, you might be reproachfully accused of what the Filipinos call "counting," which is conveniently considered to be a breach of etiquette. In other words, the Filipino translation of "loan" is "gift." If you really need the use of that money, just say "no," which is understood in most languages.

I have heard that the "forgotten loan" custom also exists in Thailand, although I did not experience it there.

Religious Differences

We come now to another important difference between Thailand and the Philippines – religion. Most Thais are Buddhist and most Filipinos are Catholic, although there are also Muslim populations in both countries.

The difference becomes significant to you in terms of getting married. The Thai government takes a secular approach to both marriage and divorce – that is, religion doesn't enter into it from a legal standpoint any more than it does in the USA. In the Philippines, however, there appears to be no separation between church and state – which is to say, Philippine marriage law follows the Catholic tradition. Counseling of the couple is required, as well as posting of the banns (a public notice of intention to marry) for 10 days prior to the marriage. You can have a civil ceremony or a church wedding, or both.

As for divorce – as of this writing, it does not exist in the Philippines, which is now the only nation in the world that bans divorce. A bill allowing divorce sits in the Philippine House of Representatives, but it is being fought hard by the powerful Catholic Church.

There is an annulment process, which is a financial bonanza for the lawyers (and possibly the judges as well). Legal costs can range from $1,000 to $5,000, the process could take anywhere from six months to three years, and even then the annulment might not be granted.

By contrast, in Thailand, if both parties agree and appear together in a district office they can get divorced in about 20 minutes. But if one party does *not* consent, the process could take up to three years.

For more information, see the chapter titled "Suppose it Doesn't Work Out?"

Saving Face

It's true: Asians care very much about saving face – or to put it the other way around, not losing face. In particular, they have a strong aversion to arguments of any kind in public. They consider it to be humiliating. This applies even if the confrontation is directed at someone else in their presence.

The Asian concern with "What will other people think?" can also extend to displays of public affection. This varies with the individual, usually depending on whether or not she has broken away from a conservative upbringing. It's best to ask first – for example, if she's meeting your flight, "May I kiss you at the airport?" She might say "sure" or maybe "just a hug" or simply, "later." The same could apply even to holding hands in public. To avoid embarrassment, ask, and respect her decision. In time she might be won over to your Western ways.

In private as well, she might show a certain restraint. After some steamy sex, don't be surprised if she wraps herself modestly with a towel en route to the shower – and that's even if you're going to shower together!

It's Better to Give

When you go to meet a girl you've been seriously corresponding with, get off to a good start by bringing a gift for her and, if she lives at home, presents for her parents. For a small gift, chocolates are a good choice – most Asians seem to like them and consider them a luxury. Higher up on the scale would be a piece of gold jewelry for the girl and a watch for each parent.

If you are meeting a girl who has agreed to spend the night with you, expect to take her shopping beforehand. Your purchases will probably involve a few articles of clothing and maybe a handbag. Try to do this at an inexpensive night market rather than a department store, where prices are often as high as in the USA.

If you expect to have sex, consider getting her agreement before the shopping trip begins. Some girls – innocently or deceitfully – will take a strictly platonic view of staying overnight, and you probably don't want to discover this when the two of you slip into bed and she says, "Good night."

Later, I'll provide more details on Thailand and the Philippines, but first let's cut to the chase – the chase for girls.

3

SOME REALITIES

The girls you'll meet are generally not as sophisticated as the well-educated American women you might be accustomed to. With few exceptions, the Asian girls I met confined their reading to restaurant menus. When I would successfully cajole one of them into my hotel room she would leap for the bed – which seemed promising – but in midair, with the deadly precision of an eagle diving onto a field mouse, she would swoop up the TV remote control and have the set lighted up before she hit the mattress.

Her programs of choice were typically the Asian versions of soap operas and game shows, plus the plethora of American movies whose artistic creativity lay in the intensity of their police chases, machinegun fire, and exploding cars.

You will get pretty good clues about the scope of their interests from their profiles on the matchmaking web sites. Mostly they express themselves as being loving and sincere and looking for the same in a man. Some also like cooking and dancing. Nothing wrong with any of that, and if you don't require a partner who will discuss world affairs or literature with you, you'll have many girls to choose from.

If you're looking for more sophistication (or at least a more polished English vocabulary), search out the women who are teachers or have upper-level jobs such as executive secretary or marketing associate.

Sometimes you'll find yourself chatting with a girl who replies to your declarations on the meaning of life – or at least the meaning of a beautiful sunset – with "ok." After a half-dozen or so of these unrewarding responses, stop rolling your eyes and gently prod her with questions that cannot reasonably be answered with "ok." For example, "Well, Moi, my favorite thing to do is swimming. What do you like to do best?" (Your real favorite thing to do might be more intimate than swimming, but that can come later.) If Moi responds with another "ok," perhaps it is best to move on.

The Little Matter of Children

Note that if you search among the girls who are in their upper 20s to lower 30s, there's a strong possibility that they are single mothers with young children, whether they admit it or not. You might welcome such a package deal, but if not, investigate carefully before you commit yourself. And be very wary of a young mother who tells you that everything's okay, her child will stay at home to be raised by grandmother. Maybe so, but I bought into that proposition and it just didn't happen as advertised.

Women in their 40s and above are likely to have grown children and that might work out all right, but remember that family ties among Asians tend to be very strong, and outstretched hands (for money, of course) can reach across an ocean.

4

HOW TO MEET THEM

When acquaintances ask me how I met my wife and I answer, "Through the Internet" I often get an "Are you kidding?" look in return. "Well," I respond, "where do you get a new camera? A toner cartridge for your printer? A Monte Python DVD? Why not a wife as well?" There is usually no answer to that.

The fact is, the easiest way to meet Asian girls (or *any* far-off girls, for that matter) is via one or more matchmaking websites. There are a number of these services but the ones that have served me best are ThaiLoveLinks.com and FilipinoCupid.com (formerly called FilipinaHeart.com). Both websites have identical formats and are easy to navigate. Their Australia-based owner also operates matchmaking sites for such ethnicities as Chinese, Japanese, Vietnamese, and more. (For the complete list, visit CupidMedia.com.)

I met many girls via ThaiLoveLinks and found my dear wife Fely through FilipinaHeart, as it was then called.

Free Membership? Well, yes, but ...

Most matchmaking sites proclaim that membership is free and that's true, in a way. At no cost, you can become a Standard member of ThaiLoveLinks and/or

FilipinoCupid, post your profile with up to five photos, and browse through the profiles of thousands of women, ranging in age from 18 to the 50s; most are in their 20s and 30s.

Each profile has the member's photo and such other information as her first name or nickname, age, location, marital status, children if any, height, weight, education, occupation, English ability, and whether she smokes, drinks, and is willing to relocate. Also, the age range she's looking for and an essay about herself and the kind of mate she is seeking.

Yes, you can check out all these women for free, but there's a major catch. Standard members cannot communicate with each other, except to send a show of interest – and, of course, all of the girls are Standard members. However, by upgrading to a Gold or Platinum membership, you can exchange messages with the girls, and they can exchange messages with you.

The Gold membership allows you to exchange on-site emails and chat with any member. At this writing, the cost for one month is $30; three months, $60; six months, $100; and 12 months, $120.

Platinum membership costs approximately 15% more and provides the additional capabilities of video mail and language translations.

The day I became a Gold member, I began to receive emails and instant messaging invitations. It's soooo nice to be sought after by lovely young ladies! But of course, you will also want to conduct your own searching, and you can do it in a variety of ways.

One method is to use the Photo Gallery function, which assembles the primary photos of all the members. Another interesting feature is the Sunshine Sweethearts Gallery, adorned by bikini-clad members displaying their charms. Click on a photo that interests you and you will be taken to that girl's profile page. You can also search by a girl's age, name, or city of residence. When I was an active member, my favorite method was to search among the girls who were currently online. I would select one who interested me and then send her a request for instant messaging via the site's IM function. If she was willing, we could then chat immediately.

Incidentally, you can expect to get IMs from ladies living in such places as Nigeria or Ghana. Ask yourself, what are they doing on a Philippine or Thai website? Answer: probably trying to scam you. I never wasted a minute with them. Also, some scammers will claim to be living in the USA. I have tested them by asking some question about their alleged city of residence, such as the name of the street they live on. Usually I got a confused answer or none at all.

You can send notes to as many girls as you want through the site's own email system. For security reasons, no personal email addresses or phone numbers are shown on the site. Once you have started corresponding, you can exchange that information.

There's another matchmaking website I think worth mentioning for those seeking a woman with strong Christian or other spiritual ties: Christian-Filipina.com. Through their Power Search function you can narrow your search to members of a particular Christian sect – Catholic, Protestant, Baptist, etc. – or to "spiritual but not religious." Also, you can broaden your search geographically to include those members who state that they now live in the USA (or any other country). On a recent day I found 92 Filipinas who said they were already here, which (if true) would eliminate overseas travel and the immigration hassle.

If you join this site, even as a non-paying member, expect almost daily emails, most with profiles of available members, others with useful language phrases and such tips as how to avoid scammers. Also, the management is very responsive to questions and concerns and can be contacted via toll-free phone, email, live chats – and their blog (christian-filipina.com/blog/), which has many articles of advice.

The paid memberships cost about the same as the other sites I mentioned previously.

The Next Step

The Instant Messaging functions on the matchmaking sites have limitations, and once you've gotten interested in a member, the next logical step is for the two of you to get to spend time together by chatting on Windows Live Messenger (often referred to by its former name, MSN) or Yahoo Instant Messenger. MSN is favored by Thais, while Filipinas prefer Yahoo. There's also Facebook's live chat feature.

You'll have to deal with a time difference of up to 16 hours, depending on which time zone you live in, but you'll probably find the immediacy and intimacy of a live chat much more satisfying than exchanges of emails.

The Webcam – Practically a Must

Best of all are webcam chats that enable you to see each other as you converse in real time. Not only do the facial expressions and body language add a great dimension to your conversations, the live cam will show you whether the girl really looks like her photos.

Speaking of photos, be wary of a profile that displays only studio shots, which are easily recognizable by the artful lighting and makeup designed to flatter the subject. If you feel yourself getting interested, ask for snapshots in natural settings. If she resists your request, have second thoughts or at least press for a webcam session. If she doesn't own a webcam, ask her to go to an Internet café that provides webcams, if only for one chat.

I feel that requests of this nature are perfectly reasonable, especially in view of the fact that if you are eventually going overseas to meet her, you will be expending a considerable outlay of money, time, and effort.

Another benefit of the webcam is that it will enable you to discover if the girl is chatting with you through a translator. You might be perfectly content with this arrangement, but the girl should be honest about her limited or non-existent English. If she is deceptive about using a translator, she will likely be devious about other things as well.

I had an amusing webcam chat with a girl I will call Gina who told me from the beginning that her girlfriend Flora was acting as translator. As the chat progressed, Flora began inserting more and more of herself into the picture – sort of like the camel sticking its nose into the tent, only she was a lot prettier than a camel, and also prettier than Gina.

On a hunch, I steered the conversation onto a path strewn with sexy innuendos and got some encouraging responses. But from whom? Gina or her flirtatious translator Flora? I found out soon enough by suggesting that I would sure like to see more of her figure, presumably referring to Gina.

The matter was settled when Flora stood up, moved behind Gina, and pulled up her blouse. All the while, Gina stared uncomprehendingly at the monitor, probably wondering why I was laughing so hard.

As it turned out, I never met either Flora or Gina.

The Cell Phone – an Absolute Must!

To an even greater degree than Americans, Asians have cell phones permanently attached to their bodies. So when you visit her country, one of your first purchases should be a cell phone that will work there. Chances are that does not include your American phone. Not to worry – you can buy one at reasonable cost overseas. (Avoid the international phone deals offered in the US. The phone might seem inexpensive, but the cost of the air time is likely to be outrageous.)

In most Asian shopping malls you will find vendors offering cell phones of all descriptions. A basic Nokia can be had for as little as $30. If you want one with built-in camera, Bluetooth and other bells and whistles, prepare to pay considerably more. My wife has an Apple iPhone, priced at about $55. That's still at the low end, pricewise, but nevertheless it lights up like a pinball machine, has animated displays, music, and might even tell your fortune.

You buy a SIM card according to the connection service you want to use. There are no monthly connection charges. Also, you are not charged airtime for calls you receive. Text messages are much cheaper than voice calls. The most popular service in Thailand is One-Two-Call; in the Philippines, it's Smart Buddy.

You pay for airtime by purchasing a phone card for 100 or 300 Thai baht or Philippine pesos. The card has a scratch-off numerical code that you enter into the phone to receive your airtime credit. Cards are available at phone shops and convenience stores.

Also, in the Philippines there are shops that can electronically load airtime into someone else's phone, which is a handy way to pick up the tab for calls from a girlfriend to you.

Meet One Girl – or More?

If all goes well (and it probably will), the time will come when you will want to meet the girl of your dreams. But it's a long, expensive trip, so you might opt to increase your chances of success by arranging to meet not just one, but several girls while you're at it. If so, should you tell each girl that you will be meeting others?

There are two schools of thought on this. Some experienced girl-hunters say "absolutely not," asserting that each girl will want to feel that she is the only one you're interested in. Their advice is to tell each one that you have to do some business while you're there, and use that as an excuse to get away and meet others. I happen to be of the old fashioned school that believes in telling the truth, and this has caused some girls to refuse to meet me. So be it – it's a matter of personal ethics.

If you have your heart set on only one girl, hopefully it's based on countless hours of webcam chats, phone calls, emails, and perhaps some gifts. Go forth to meet that one girl, but I strongly suggest that you bring a file of runners-up ... just in case.

Local Introduction Services

In addition to the major online services, there are the so-called personalized introduction services that operate out of local offices abroad. The proprietors claim to save you heartache by carefully screening their girls as to their character and thus help prevent such unpleasant surprises as undisclosed boyfriends, children, or even husbands.

I used two of these services in Thailand and found their screening to be faulty or non-existent. In other words, girls I met turned out to be not as advertised. In hindsight, it was unrealistic to expect any business short of a private detective agency to be able to provide such in-depth investigations. Therefore, I am mentioning these services simply as a warning to use them with caution, if at all.

The Good Old-Fashioned Pickup

If you're truly adventurous and have time and money to spare, you could just hop a plane to the country of your choice, set up headquarters in a likely city, and do your girl-shopping in person.

For starters, many sizeable cities have very nice shopping malls, often under the banner of the Robinsons chain of department stores. (The chain now bears the Macys name in the USA, but it's still Robinsons abroad.)

I have been to a number of these malls in both Thailand and the Philippines and I couldn't help noticing that many of the salesgirls are quite attractive and well educated, with a good command of the English language. A lot of the large companies require their sales girls to have associate degrees and, better yet, to be single.

Here is a pickup technique that I haven't used but have read about in a couple of sources and it sounds like it would be worth trying: The idea is to approach a likely prospect – for example, an attractive salesgirl – when there is nobody else within earshot, explain to her that you are single, and ask if she would become your text buddy.

If she agrees she will give you her cell phone number and the two of you can communicate by sending text messages back and forth until you can get her to the next level. Text messaging is a good way to ease into a relationship. Both of you can receive and reply to them at convenient times. Also, it is a lot cheaper than voice calls, which is likely to be important to the girl. In fact, you can load some air time onto her phone so she doesn't have any expense.

Even if she's not interested in you for herself, she might have a relative, friend, or co-worker who is dying to meet a nice American, so carry some slips of paper to hand out, on which you've written your first name and cell phone number.

The Personal Reference

This method is largely a matter of happenstance – a local Asian family who might know of a good, honest girl overseas – or better yet, right here in the USA. You don't know an Asian family? Think again. What about that Thai restaurant or Asian food market that you patronize regularly (or can start doing so tomorrow) and have become friendly with the staff? Nothing wrong with letting them know that you respect their culture so much that you would be honored to have one of them as your wife. In fact, if you offer that confidence to the pretty young girl behind the cash register she might blush and hand you her cell phone number!

Purely a matter of luck, you say? Maybe, but remember, a lot of "lucky" people in this world make their own luck – and it doesn't hurt to ask.

5

IF SHE ASKS FOR $$$

At some point in your correspondence the girl might ask you for money. Some of the Internet dating services warn about this and they strongly advise members never to send money to other members they haven't met.

I can't quarrel with this advice – a lot of women are out to get money from as many men as possible, and, in fact, some of them might not even be women; after all, anybody can post a photo of an attractive girl and create a phony profile. However, on a couple of occasions I have disregarded this advice, with varying results.

One of my early Internet contacts was with a Thai member named Polla. After a few warm Internet chats we agreed that on my next visit to Thailand I would take her to the resort island of Phuket. I made this offer rather foolishly because she had already aroused my suspicions when she requested a monthly allowance to cover the Internet café charges for her chats. This in itself was not unreasonable, but I knew the typical hourly café charges and the amount she wanted would have kept her chatting on the Internet for eight hours a day, seven days a week, possibly with a bunch of my rivals.

The capper came when she asked for a sum of money to pay for airfare to Bangkok – plus two days of hotel and meal expenses – in order to obtain a passport for our trip to Phuket. A passport to travel within her own country? It didn't make sense, but just to be sure I checked with the Thai Embassy, and either Polla wasn't very bright or, more likely, she didn't think I was, so it was goodbye Polla.

I never sent Polla a dime but I wasn't so smart with Ann – a really cute young girl, if her photos were to be believed. Ann wanted $50 because her mother needed an operation. I hadn't yet learned that "mother needs an operation" is a favorite money story, so I sent the $50. Wouldn't you know, the day after she received the $50, Ann gave me the heart-rending news that as she was boarding a bus from the bank, a thief grabbed her purse and ran off with the money. I told Ann that she had my sympathy but I was not sending another $50. She dropped me instantly.

Conversely, I sent some aid to a girl in the Philippines and it was money well spent. She had not asked me for anything, but by this time I was well aware that most Asian families are financially stressed and I wanted to help because I had a powerful intuition that this was the girl for me. My intuition was right and now she is my wife. She still mentions how surprised and impressed she was that I volunteered my assistance before we met.

So it's a judgment call and my advice is to be on the alert for scams but also be open to providing some assistance to a girl who seems right for you. Chances are her response will give you a clue as to her character.

6

SUPPOSE IT DOESN'T WORK OUT?

You've tried your best, maybe she has, too. But you've decided that you were crazy to have been crazy about her, and hopefully she shares your sentiment. How do you untie the knot that binds you to a foreigner?

If you haven't gotten married it could be simple or it could become a problem, depending on where she is located. If you *have* gotten married, a lot will depend on the laws in her country and yours. Let's look at some examples of what might happen if the relationship goes south.

Three Scenarios

Scenario #1: She's here on a fiancée visa and you haven't married her yet. Sounds like a no-brainer. Under the terms of the fiancée visa, if you don't marry within 90 days of her entry into the USA she is required to return to her country. But suppose she refuses to go home? Suppose, in fact, her real reason for hooking up with you was to get to the United States? You can't physically force her to get on a plane, and calling 911 is not likely to help – it's not their department. What about the Immigration authorities? Not much help there, either – at least, not in my unfortunate experience with a Thai fiancée named Nan. I'll tell you more about that in the chapter titled "My Two Fiancée Visas."

So if you bring the girl of your dreams from her place to your place, you're taking something of a risk if the dream becomes a nightmare. But all relationships have risks; it's just that the fiancée visa has its own kind of risk.

Of course, if you marry her in the USA, you're both subject to the divorce laws of the state in which you reside.

Scenario #2: You've gotten married in her country and you've brought her here on a spousal visa. Even though the marriage took place abroad it will be recognized as valid and binding in the USA and its dissolution will be governed by the laws of your state of residence.

Scenario #3: The two of you are married and still in her country, in which case you are both theoretically subject to the laws of that country. However, as a foreigner you have the advantage of being able to say "bye-bye" and go home, and without a visa she can't follow you. So let's say she's a Thai and she demands an outrageous settlement to participate in a quickie Thai divorce. A good response is, "Fine, I'll just go home and stop supporting you." That will probably persuade her to be more reasonable.

The Prenuptial Agreement

A "prenup," as the lawyers call it, is a legal contract in which each of you itemizes your assets and both of you agree on a financial settlement if the marriage should end in a separation or divorce.

Your list of assets would include the current value of your bank accounts, CDs, stocks, bonds, real estate, and other property. Her list would probably be short to non-existent. Your purpose in having a prenup is to protect your assets, particularly if your marriage breaks up after she has been living with you in the US.

A local lawyer should be able to advise you of a prenup's degree of protection according to the court practices in your state. The lawyer will probably stress the importance of your fiancée fully understanding the document she is signing if it is to have any validity later on – and for that reason, the prenup should ideally be written in her native language as well as English, and she should be represented by someone who is fluent in her language.

You might feel some embarrassment about asking your fiancée to participate in an agreement on the terms of a breakup before you are even married, but as long as the prenup includes some financial benefit for her, as it should, you can point out that it is for her protection as well as yours.

Other Safeguards

Regardless of whom you marry, or even if you remain single, you should consider executing certain documents to make sure that your wishes are carried out in the event of your serious illness or death.

For example, an advanced health care directive (also known as a living will) enables you to name an individual to make medical decisions in your behalf if you become incapable of doing so. This includes your preference about maintaining life support in the event of a terminal condition.

You might also want to create a revocable trust that will have title to all of your valuable assets, including your bank accounts and real estate. This avoids the time-consuming and costly probate process of an ordinary will.

7

SEX WITHOUT MARRIAGE

While the prime purpose of this book is to help you find the right girl to marry, it is certainly possible to meet nice, respectable Asian girls for companionship (yes, including sex) that doesn't result in marriage. I did a lot of wife-shopping and during my many visits to Thailand I ate, played and slept with women ranging in age from 19 to 40. Some were teachers, one was a college student, others were farm girls.

I was straightforward with all of them, explaining that I was definitely looking for a wife and also making it clear that I was planning on meeting others during these trips. I did not make any phony protestations of love or offers of marriage in order to obtain sexual favors.

While the girls I met were also sincere in seeking marriage, I found that most of them were quite willing to have sex without a marriage commitment, especially if they were treated to a few days at a nice resort, a luxury many had never enjoyed.

I'll tell you about some of my adventures and misadventures later in this chapter, but certainly you could go for immediate gratification simply by picking up a bar girl, aka prostitute. I never did that. I was overseas to find a wife, and although some Americans and other foreigners marry bar girls, I have never so much as bought one an overpriced beer.

However, if you want to venture into paid sex, you'll find plenty of it in Thailand and the Philippines. Although prostitution is theoretically illegal in both countries, it is winked at by the authorities.

Bangkok's sex trade attracts a lot of horny visitors, with most of the action taking place in a well-defined red-light district. I have heard that tourists can get ripped off there in scary ways and it is probably safest to get a reliable guide whose tours include this type of recreation.

Bar girls also abound in such tourist magnets as Pattaya and Phuket's major city of Patong. In the Philippines, a high concentration of rent-a-girls can be found in Manila, Angeles City, Puerto Galera, Davao, and Cebu.

Incidentally, it is often said of bar girls that they ply their trade in order to provide the financial necessities for their families. Why are the families in such desperate need? Often it is because the father has run off with some other woman, but possibly more often good old Dad – or maybe the girl's husband – is at home sitting on his butt and seriously engaged in drinking and gambling with like-minded friends. If these so-called heads of the family feel any shame in allowing their girl to become the breadwinner by spreading her legs, they manage to live with it.

A word of advice: If you want a woman, make sure at the outset that a woman is what you're really getting. For example, to see some stunning beauties, Google the Miss Ladyboy pageant in Phuket. Ladyboys, i.e., transvestites, seem to be an especially vibrant part of the Thai culture.

Sex with Underage Girls

Sex with a minor in the USA is risky, as you probably know, and it can be even more perilous in Thailand and the Philippines, where a criminal defendant's civil rights are less strictly observed. Even though prostitution flourishes openly in those countries, the governments are righteously protective of underage girls. Penalties for sex with minors can result in fines and lengthy imprisonment, so beware of having a relationship, even unwittingly, with a girl under the age of 18.

I learned about such a case from a Thai matchmaker, whose American customer became engaged to a girl who had stated that she was 18. In the course of getting to know her (in the Biblical sense and otherwise) he discovered that she had some unacceptable habits and broke off the engagement. At this point the mother revealed (maybe even truthfully) that the girl was really only 17 and demanded a large payment, aka blackmail, to let the guy off the hook. He paid. So if you have any intentions on a sweet young thing, demand to see her I.D. and hope it is genuine. Better yet, confine yourself to girls who are obviously at least in their 20s.

Another matchmaker of my acquaintance offered to get me an hour with a 15-year-old schoolgirl for 3000 baht, about $100. I was told I could choose from a lineup of three classmates and could probably negotiate a special price for all three if I was pumped up for it. I declined the offer.

This gentleman also told me that, for his own pleasure, he rented a pristine 17-year-old girl from her father, also for 3000 baht – a real bargain because it was for an entire week. As a precaution, he had the father sign a contract – sort of like a Hertz rental agreement, only she had no mileage on her – and he later sent me a nice family photo of himself, the girl, and Dad, seated together on the living room sofa.

The girl looked cute and was smiling for the camera. It was not clear whether she knew at the time how she would be kept busy during the coming week. Dad looked serious, but I don't think it was because of his conscience.

Shortly after this experience the girl became a prostitute, which shows what can be accomplished by home schooling.

Personal Experiences

Here are a few of my escapades in Thailand, mostly embarked on via ThaiLoveLinks. (The stories are true but the girls' names are not.) In some cases there was sex, other times I came up empty. Some of the occasions involved stupidity and/or insensitivity on my part, with the unfortunate outcomes I richly deserved.

Liu

I had told Liu I would be arriving on a certain flight to her home town of Udon Thani, where I was to meet several girls at my hotel of choice, the Grand Royal. I arrived as scheduled and was on the shuttle van from the airport to the hotel when my cell phone rang. It was Liu, very disappointed because she had planned to surprise me by meeting me at the airport but she had arrived a little late and now she wanted to come to my hotel. I agreed and she showed up in a truck driven by Santo, the owner of a resort where her mother worked.

Liu was rather plain but a nice, agreeable girl. I asked if she would like to spend the night with me and she assented, so Santo drove off. We had sex that night but she would not allow me to kiss her. I had heard that some Asian girls do not like kissing but this was my first experience of sex with no kissing.

The next morning I asked if she would spend more time with me and she said she would, but she wanted me to stay with her at Santo's resort, where I could meet her mother, so we went there.

Liu's mother was very cordial to me. The resort consisted of a group of small bungalows situated by a lake. I did not care much for the place. Although the lake was scenic, the accommodations were very cramped – especially the closet-like bathroom that did not even have a sink. After a couple of days of this, I offered to take Liu to Phuket for a week but her mother was cautious and said I could take her on my next visit.

There did not seem to be an immediate expectation of marriage, which relieved me because although Liu and I got along nicely I did not feel that we had much in common. I returned to the Grand Royal.

Incidentally, although Liu and I had sex each time we were together, I never was able to convince her to let me kiss her.

May

May was a member of a hill tribe in Chiang Rai. Her photos showed her to be a very attractive girl with a nice slender figure, and the webcam confirmed that. Our chats went nicely until May's aunt, with whom May lived, thrust herself into the picture literally and figuratively. She began to sit next to May – not participating in the chats but evidently looking me over with considerable interest.

This reached its climax when May announced that her aunt wanted me and therefore she would have to step aside in favor of her elderly relative. Well, perhaps May didn't have a choice, but I did, and I informed May that I was not interested in her aunt. At that point, May terminated our relationship – I suppose in order to save face for her aunt – and I reluctantly crossed her off my list.

However, during my next visit to Thailand, I impulsively called May and asked to see her. To my delight, she agreed and I took the next flight to Chiang Mai, where May was visiting at the time. After a nice dinner at a riverside restaurant we went to the city's well-known night market, where I bought a few things for May. Then it was on to our hotel and to bed, where May posed the unnecessary question, "Do you want to have sex?"

The next morning we went to one of Chiang Mai's elephant parks, where we saw the pachyderms perform and had an hour-long elephant ride on a hilly, uneven trail, lurching in all directions. Throughout our time together, I enjoyed May's outgoing personality and we discussed the possibility of marriage.

She asked for a modest dowry. I forget the amount but what I do remember is that it was just a down payment because she also required that I send her aunt support money in the amount of 10,000 baht, or $300-plus, each month.

I told her that I felt that this was rather steep just for one family member. Her immediate response was to ask if I had a friend who would replace me – presumably to the tune of the $300-plus a month. I answered "no" and a chill factor set in. She spent a second night with me but soon after we went to bed I discovered that I had disqualified myself from further sex.

Nana

I met Nana during another visit to Chiang Mai. It had been arranged that she would spend the night with me but when she met me at the airport with a girlfriend, I wondered if we would be a *ménage a troi*, that is, three in a bed. This would have been fine with me, as both girls were very pretty. However, our threesome was limited to dinner in a Japanese restaurant where Nana worked. Afterwards, the girlfriend left and Nana and I went to bed as a twosome, with the anticipated results.

The next morning, I invited Nana to use the pool but she said she had no swimsuit. So, of course, I bought her a swimsuit. We spent some time relaxing by the pool and then Nana excused herself for what I thought would be a brief trip to the restroom. However, after some time had passed and she had not reappeared, I went to the room. She was not there. I phoned her and she told me she'd had to leave for a while but would be back later. She never returned. Obviously, I had not interested her and she had chosen this rather indirect way of letting me know.

Ani

I met Ani over lunch in the restaurant of Udon Thani's Grand Royal. Not surprisingly, she brought family representatives, consisting of her mom, who spoke no English, and her aunt, who spoke English quite well. Ani's English was limited, but she eventually taught me a word that had great significance.

When I first set eyes on Ani, I groaned to myself. She was a little thing, wore braces, and could have passed for 15. A shy and serious-looking 15. As we ate, the aunt informed me that Ani had taken the day off from work to meet me and therefore it was my responsibility to take care of her for the rest of the day.

At this, my groan was almost audible. I steeled myself by calling upon the philosophy that sustains me in times like these: *You win some and you lose some. That is life, especially with women.*

The relatives departed and I took Ani to my room. Take care of her for the rest of the day? What was I going to do with her? The answer came quickly and delightfully. I made a perfunctory pass, her shyness vanished, and in a flash we were between the sheets.

She proved to be an enthusiastic bed partner – so much so that I invited her to a week in Phuket. She accepted readily. It turned out that her job was with a family business and was only temporary, as she would soon be enrolling in Bangkok University.

We filled that week very nicely. Oh, about the word she taught me. When I would guide her toward the bed she would say, "Oh, you want boom-boom." Or sometimes, "No boom-boom now. Later." Subsequently, I heard other girls use the word. Do I need to define it for you?

Maybelle

I met Maybelle, a farm girl, in the lobby of my usual headquarters, the Grand Royal. She was tall and very attractive. She came alone, which was a nice surprise, and soon we were in my room, getting well acquainted by means of energetic foreplay, when her cell phone rang and she announced that mama needed her for some farm chores. Pausing only for some hasty buttoning-up she was out the door.

I don't think this was just an excuse to leave, because I had agreed to take her shopping afterwards, but the wishes of mama are never to be disregarded in the Thai culture. Not being a big fan of *coitus interruptus*, I did not contact her again.

Nek

I met Nek in Udon Thani in the lobby of – you guessed it – the Grand Royal. She had a nice face and a very good figure. She spoke little English but she made it clear that she wanted me to meet her mother and sister, who were at the Robinsons mall. We walked over and I was introduced. The mother spoke no English at all, but the sister's English was considerably better than Nek's. Sis told me that she and Mom were about to eat. This was followed by a significant silence. I did the expected and invited them all to dinner.

As the extensive meal began winding down, I asked Sis, who was conducting most of our conversation, if Nek would care to spend the night with me. "Yes," came the answer after a brief huddle, "but she has nothing with her." Another significant silence.

Veteran actor that I was, I picked up my cue. "Of course, we'll get whatever she needs." Sis and Mom went their way. Our way was to a drugstore, where Nek headed unerringly for the makeup department. There followed numerous purchases of facial creams, powders, eyeliners, lipstick – in short, everything a girl needs to stay overnight. Almost as an afterthought, she added a toothbrush.

Of course, we weren't done yet, as Nek had no change of clothing. I was spared buying a complete wardrobe – in fact, Nek considerately settled for a new shirt. The total for everything, including the dinner, was about $60. *It could have been worse,* I told myself. Well, it was going to get worse.

We got to my room and sat on the bed. I kissed her a couple of times and was gratified when her tongue ventured demurely into my mouth. I asked if she would like to shower. "After you," she replied politely.

I showered. I came back into the room. It didn't take long for me to notice that I was the only one there. Nek had vanished into the night, along with her newly acquired makeup and shirt. A profitable evening for Nek, and all it cost her were two kisses.

I sent her a brief text message, expressing some reflections on her disappearing act. I did not expect a reply and in this regard Nek met my expectations. I guess the moral is: *shower afterwards.*

Karl

Our first online chat rather quickly got around to sex. She said to me that she would be interested in learning to perform oral sex if I would teach her. Needless to say, I was more than willing to oblige. The bad news was that she did not want to have penile sex because she had tried it once with a woman friend (presumably using a device designed for that purpose) and the woman had hurt her. Well, I thought, half a bushel is better than none, so I agreed to the compromise.

At her suggestion I reserved a cottage at a resort on the island of Koh Chang. The place was called Seaview Resort and it was quite nice even though only a few of the cottages had a view of the sea.

As promised, I taught her to perform (and receive) oral sex. She was an apt pupil and I was a happy teacher. As for penile sex, she stuck to her guns and I did not press the matter. However, I made the mistake of saying something intemperate to her in a public place and that was the end of our relationship.

If this is beginning to sound familiar, take heed: if you have something of a short fuse, keep a lid on it when you are with an Asian lady. A display of temper, particularly in a public place, is never acceptable. If you are thinking, "Hey, it's not acceptable even in the United States," I won't argue the point.

Lana

Lana taught computer science to high school students. We established a friendly online relationship and she agreed to spend most of her summer vacation with me – actually, the first week with me in Phuket, the second week with a female co-worker at an inexpensive resort mainly for Thais, and back to me in Phuket for the third week.

She was on the plump side, not a head-turning beauty, but pleasant-looking and very intelligent. I was somewhat put off, however, midway in the first week when we got into a discussion of dowries. She had two married sisters and she told me that the first sister received a dowry of 1 million baht, while the second sibling was awarded no less than 5 million baht – that's upwards of $33,000 and $165,000 respectively! And the husbands were Thais, not foreigners.

Either Lana was embroidering the truth or she was swimming in a social circle that was too rich for my blood. It turned out that *I* was too rich for *her* blood in another way. At the end of our holiday she advised me that sex every morning was a lot more than she cared for. If she had mentioned this at the time, I certainly would have respected her wishes, but I thought she was enjoying it as much as I was. Anyway, we remained friends for a long time.

June

June was a teacher in Bangkok, age 30 and quite pretty. During one of our webcam chats she had just gotten out of bed and "absent-mindedly" took off her nightgown, revealing everything Nature had blessed her with. Then, "remembering" that she was on camera she gave an unconvincing demonstration of embarrassment. I was so horrified at this display of forgetfulness that I could hardly wait to meet her.

When I arrived in Bangkok, I booked a room at a riverside hotel near her school. It was a Hilton, and therefore quite expensive by Thai or any other standards, but worth a splurge for a few days. One of the amenities was a unique rooftop pool where the chaises sat in a shallow part of the water. The view of the river and the city beyond was quite spectacular.

June showed up after her teaching hours and on the second night as we were heading for bed, I managed to come up with one of my fatal mistakes. My cell phone rang and the caller was Ani. Instead of letting my voicemail handle the call, I answered the phone, and worse yet, wandered into the bathroom to have a private conversation. I kept it short, but it was long enough for me to discover June hastily and angrily dressing. I apologized profusely, but she was gone without so much as a goodbye.

I finally began to get the message that where Thai girlfriends are concerned there is little margin for mistakes – or at least, *my* kind of mistakes.

Poona

Following is a transcript of our online chat, and I am not making this up:

Poona: I am 56 years old.

Me: Your profile says 44.

Poona: My daughter typed my profile for me.

Me: Earlier you said you can type English well.

Poona: Yes.

Me: Also, your profile says you have no children.

Poona: I forgot.

Me: You forgot your children?

Poona: Yes.

Me: Is your daughter typing our chat?

Poona: Yes.

Me: I think she has a short memory.

Poona: Sorry.

I decided not to pursue a relationship with Poona.

Well, there you have the stories of some of my ups and downs (figuratively and sometimes literally) with Thai girls. I have no similar anecdotes involving Filipinas because the only girl I met in the Philippines was the one who showed me that I need look no further, my wife Fely.

8

TAKING OR SENDING MONEY ABROAD

In this chapter I'll discuss how to help keep your valuables secure while traveling, along with various ways to send money overseas. Let's begin with some basics on the currencies of Thailand and the Philippines.

The Thai currency is called the baht (TBT). At this writing, one baht is worth about three and a third cents. Thus, for example, 100 baht equals approximately $3.33 and one dollar is worth a little over 30 baht. Commonly used coins are in denominations of 1, 5, and 10 baht. Paper currency comes in denominations of 10, 20, 50, 100, 500, and 1,000 baht.

The Philippine currency is the peso (PHP). At this writing, one peso is worth about two and a half cents. Thus, for example, 100 pesos equals approximately $2.50 and one dollar is worth about 40 pesos. Commonly used coins are in denominations of 1, 5, and 10 pesos. Paper currency comes in denominations of 10, 20, 50, 100, 200, 500, and 1,000 pesos.

For up-to-date conversion rates of virtually any country's currency, visit one of the online converters, such as themoneyconverter.com.

Traveling with Money

When you're traveling anywhere, obviously you won't want to carry a lot of cash that might be lost or stolen. Whatever valuables and identification you do carry should be made as secure as possible, especially from pickpockets. I keep my valuables in a zippered nylon security pouch, which has two belt loops and is tucked inside my pants. It costs $9.45 at magellans.com, a company that offers several other types of security wallets, along with many other travel aids.

Another company I've used, travelseal.com, sells security wallets, luggage locks, and other anti-theft products.

When I began my travels to Thailand I carried most of the funds I expected to need (plus a healthy margin for unexpected expenses) in American Express traveler's checks, but I soon found this to be a nuisance. The checks could be converted into baht at banks and money-changing kiosks, but the agents took photocopies of my passport and usually would phone my hotel to make sure I was a guest there, and the whole business took a lot of time – plus there was a fee per check in addition to their conversion rate.

My experience was even worse in the Philippines. The one time I needed to cash a traveler's check I went to a bank and was sent to the manager. She wanted to see the receipt for my purchase of the check, which I did not have with me. After much discussion, she reluctantly initialed a form, which I then had to take to the end of a slow-moving line that led eventually to a teller.

Your credit cards will be of limited use in either country. They are accepted at most hotels. Some shops, restaurants, tour operators, etc. will take Visa and MasterCard – seldom any other kind – and they will usually add a surcharge of 3-5%. Most credit card issuers will also charge a fee for foreign transactions, generally about 3%.

The solution that has worked best for me has been the ATM card. There are ATM machines throughout both Thailand and the Philippines. You'll want to be sure to get a card that's widely accepted in the country you're visiting, and you'll also want to know if your bank charges a transaction fee.

For my Thailand trips, I used a Visa ATM card issued by the bank where I have my checking account, but that bank subsequently sent me one of those letters beginning with, "We value you as a customer," which invariably translates into "Here comes another shafting" – in this case, a 3% fee on foreign ATM transactions.

This is a form of tough love I can do without, so when my travels subsequently began taking me to the Philippines, I looked around and found that MetLife Bank, the banking arm of the Metropolitan Life Insurance Company, did not charge a fee for ATM transactions anywhere. Although not every Philippine ATM machine accepted my card, several major Philippine banks with machines throughout the country did accept it for their maximum withdrawal of 10,000 pesos (about $250) per transaction and I could do two successive transactions in a day.

While MetLife Bank didn't charge a fee, most of the overseas banks that own the ATM machines charge their own fee of 200 pesos per transaction, which amounts to a 2% surcharge on 10,000 pesos. The fee is fixed at 200 pesos regardless of the amount of the withdrawal, so you might as well draw the maximum amount each time.

Update: MetLife sold its banking operation to GE Retail Bank (GERB) and the transition was completed on Jan. 14, 2013. A customer service representative of

GERB assured me that the services provided by Metlife Bank will remain the same, but I've heard that song before, so who knows what the future will bring. GERB's website is gogecapital.com.

If you go the ATM route, check with the issuing bank to see if you need to notify them when you're traveling abroad. I learned this the hard way when I arrived in Bangkok and put my VISA card into an ATM machine at the airport. The machine informed me that the card was not valid and then swallowed it.

This was not a good beginning for my trip. I had to get a manager to open the machine and rescue my card. There followed a series of tense and expensive phone calls to my bank in California. It turned out that VISA's ever-vigilant fraud department saw a foreign transaction about to take place and apparently decided that nobody in their right mind would travel outside the good old USA, so somehow a thief in Thailand must have gotten hold of my card (*and* pin code), and it would be really smart to invalidate the card.

Never mind what this would do to their customer if he was depending on it for travel expenses. Fortunately, I had an emergency backup consisting of $500 in traveler's checks, which I still carry during my travels.

Sending Money Overseas

If you want to help your overseas lady with an occasional gift of money, you can wire it there quickly through one of several services. The best known one, Western Union, has agencies at many banks, supermarkets, and drug stores. Your gal can receive cash "in minutes" in US dollars, or the currency of her country, at a local Western Union agency. WU's lowest fee is currently $5 for wiring amounts up to $50; for sending larger amounts, higher fee levels start at $12.50. Bear in mind that if she is paid in her country's currency, Western Union will make a profit in the conversion (they don't tell you how much), so you might want to add something extra to cover the money that will fall through the cracks.

MoneyGram offers same-day service to both Thailand and the Philippines. If you pay cash for the transaction, the fee is $9.95. If you use a credit card, the fee is $14.

Xoom.com provides online service to a number of countries including the Philippines but not Thailand. Their fee is $4.99 for sending any amount below $3000 by electronic withdrawal from your bank account. If you pay by debit or credit card, the fee is $5.99, plus any fee your credit card company might assess. I saw Internet postings from some customers who are happy with the service and others who complained that after providing service for a long time, xoom suddenly refused to continue serving them and would not provide an explanation. Xoom wouldn't provide an explanation to me either, when I queried them about these complaints.

Remithome.com provides service to the Philippines, charging a fee of $10 for any amount up to $1000, or $8 for recurring weekly or monthly transfers. These fees are for transfers from your bank; credit and debit card transfers cost $25. The funds can be deposited into the recipient's bank account, held for pickup, or delivered door-to-door at no extra charge.

You can send money by PayPal for a fee as low as 25 cents. The recipient can receive the money through a linked bank account, or can request a check, or can have the funds applied to a PayPal debit card. I use a PayPal account for some purchases and I have never had a problem. However, on the community forum on PayPal's own website, some users are threatening a class action suit against PayPal, alleging that the company has delayed making payments for long periods of time.

You can also have your bank wire the money, customarily at a flat fee of $40, but she will need her own bank account to receive it, and her bank might also charge a fee. Or you can mail personal checks to her, but be aware that her bank will place a hold of four to six weeks on a foreign check. Also, overseas mail service adds even more time and can be unreliable. Incidentally, International Postal Money Orders are not valid in either Thailand or the Philippines.

I knew a man who regularly sent cash by mail – a $50 bill or two sandwiched between some photographs – but of course he was gambling that the money would not be "lost" en route.

My Choice for Regular Transfers

If your relationship is sound enough that you will be sending support money on a regular basis, a cheap, fast, and reliable method is to give her an ATM card linked to an account that you can fund from the US. When I married Fely I opened a second MetLife (now GERB) savings account with its own ATM card, which I gave to her so she would have funds in the Philippines while awaiting her visa. Each month, I went online and instantaneously transferred her allowance from my account into hers. Also, I could fund either account from checking and savings accounts I had in other banks. (Transfers from one bank to another must be set up ahead of time.)

It's generally wise to send no more than one month's allowance at a time, because larger amounts are likely to disappear – often into the outstretched hands of relatives.

9

GETTING THERE

Whether you're flying to Thailand or the Philippines, there's a tremendous disparity in fares among the various airlines, and I mean a difference of up to $3000 round trip – and that's in economy class! Other price swings will take place at different times of the year, with the fares peaking during holidays that occur in both the US and the destination countries.

To determine which airline is currently offering the best combination of low fare and acceptable schedule, I plug my travel dates into orbitz.com. Using their information on available flights I then visit the websites of the airlines whose fares and schedules seem most attractive.

Usually I'll end up booking directly with the airline, rather than through a travel agent, for the following reasons: (1) Airlines nowadays seem very desirous of avoiding commissions or discounts to agencies and are thus offering their best prices online. Note: those prices are considerably higher if you book by phone.

(2) Some airlines offer different classes of ticketing, even within their economy fares. For example, the cheapest fare might restrict your stay to 30 days; the next upgrade could increase it to six months. You can

check out these details on the airlines' websites and you're not likely to learn about them anywhere else. You'll also learn if there's a penalty for making changes after you book.

(3) If you do have to change your flight arrangements and you've booked through a travel agent, some airlines will make you re-book through the agent, who might charge you additionally for the service.

Bottom line: If you don't want to be bothered by shopping the different airlines, book through a good travel agent. Conversely, if you're willing to spend a little time and effort checking prices and schedules, you'll probably improve your chances of booking the flights that best meet your needs.

Coping with Long Distance Flights

Twelve to 20 hours on a plane, particularly in economy class, can be quite literally a pain in the butt, as well as in the neck and various other body parts. I have even less padding than those economy seats, so I bring along an inflatable seat cushion, as well as a neck cushion to keep my head from flopping over as I sleep (or try to).

Most neck cushions have a horse-collar shape and I've tried them, but the one that works best for me, called the Travel Nook, has two connected inflatable cushions that cradle my head very comfortably. Inflatable lumbar cushions are also available, as well as inflatable or folding footrests. These products, and more, can be obtained through magellans.com.

My other equipment includes a sleep mask and ear plugs, the latter to diminish (it never completely silences) the shrill screams of the disgruntled baby who is always located too close to me — that is, on the same airplane.

Then there's the question of which is better, a window seat or an aisle seat? The benefit of an aisle seat is that you can readily use the lavatory or just stretch your body (highly recommended every few hours) without climbing over other passengers. However, those other passengers might then be climbing over you. If you're in a window seat, you'll have to do the climbing, but at least nobody will be disturbing your rest.

My preference has settled on the aisle seat, primarily for the ease of getting up to use the lavatory and – well worth considering – to avoid the possibility of a blood clot caused by remaining in a sitting position for a very long time. (Yes, it's a rare occurrence, but why risk it?)

One way to reduce the fatigue of a long flight is to book a flight that has a change of planes along the way, as is often the case. The stopover will give you a chance to really stretch yourself, get some relief from the confining atmosphere of the airborne cattle car, and if your frequent flier status gives you access to a VIP lounge, enjoy a comfortable chair and a snack while awaiting your connecting flight.

Having said that, I prefer to sit through a nonstop flight and get it over with. This not only reduces the chance of my checked baggage going astray, it also eliminates the possibility of missing a connecting flight because the originating flight arrived late. It happened to me once, and Cathay Pacific had to put me up at a Tokyo hotel that was horrendously expensive (they all are in Tokyo) and feed me a couple of equally pricey meals. It was kind of fun, especially as I was not picking up the tab, but my preference would have been to arrive on schedule.

In the more detailed chapters on Thailand and the Philippines I'll describe the methods of travel to and within those countries.

10

HOTEL OR CONDO?

At some point during your meeting with your girl (maybe the first day if all goes well) the two of you will want to stay together. The most convenient place will be a local hotel. The next step up will be a nice resort. Another choice is a condo rental.

Let's start with some hotel information.

A room in a nice hotel in a small city can be had for as little as $35 a day. Rates in big cities such as Bangkok and Manila run from $45 to $90 for a satisfactory hotel on up to $150 or more for the grander places. The quoted prices generally include the VAT (Value Added Tax) of 10-12%, but some establishments add this to your total tab, along with a 15-17% service charge, so inquire before you book, to avoid unpleasant surprises. Many hotels offer a free breakfast, consisting of both Asian and American dishes.

Visa and MasterCard are widely accepted, with a lower batting average for American Express.

To search out a hotel, you can use such online booking agencies as AsiaRooms.com, Agoda.com, and Sawasdee.com. They will show most, if not all, the hotels in major cities and resort areas, and their listings include rates, photos of the facilities and reviews by past guests.

I find the reviews very helpful. I won't be unduly influenced by one review, but if several guests complain about rude service, lack of cleanliness, or noise from an adjacent disco, I'll take their word for it and search elsewhere.

You can book your room through these agencies, using a Visa or MasterCard, and in most cases you'll get a lower rate than if you book directly with the hotel of your choice.

When you make a reservation, whether directly through the hotel or through an agency, be sure you understand their reservation and cancellation policies. For example, will you be required to prepay for the entire length of your stay, and if so, what is your obligation if you cancel before you arrive or if you decide you don't like the hotel when you get there?

The policies vary widely. For example, you can book directly at the Grand Royal in Thailand and the Leyte Park Hotel in the Philippines without paying in advance. By contrast, Thailand's Kata Poolside requires advance payment for the entire length of your stay and that payment is not refundable.

Policies also very among the agencies. AsiaRooms requires complete prepayment, while Agoda does not. Prepayment does give you some assurance that you will have the accommodations you want at the rate you arranged for. Of course, nothing is 100% certain and there are occasions where guests arrive to find that the type of room they booked is not available and, worse yet, the entire hotel is full. I have seen these stories in some of the hotel reviews, but in all my travels it has never happened to me. Yet.

How About a Condo?

If you are planning to remain in one location for a week or more, you might consider renting a condo, which is often advertised as a villa. You will have all the comforts of home – two or three bedrooms, probably two bathrooms, a living room, kitchen, and dining area. Chances are you won't need more than one bedroom (at least, I *hope* not!) but all this living space can be yours for less than you might pay for a typical hotel room. Other amenities sometimes include a sun deck and even a private swimming pool.

Possible downsides: The location might not be as advantageous as a hotel for shopping, beach, etc. You probably will not have maid service, although that is sometimes available as an option. Perhaps most important, if something goes wrong, you are dependent on a local manager to fix it, which might take some time. So if you want a totally carefree vacation and don't wish to do any cooking or cleaning, a hotel is probably the better choice.

Still, if the two of you get serious, a love nest with kitchen facilities will serve as a good rehearsal for the home life to come. It will also give you a chance to find out if she can cook!

11

GIRL-HUNTING IN THAILAND

In this chapter and the one that follows I'm going to provide useful information on visiting Thailand and the Philippines, respectively, in search of girlfriends and/or a wife. I'll use Los Angeles as a departure point because I live near there. Your mileage may vary.

I consider both countries to be very much alike in many ways, but there are also some significant differences. Although both are poor, relative to Western countries, Thailand has a somewhat stronger economy than the Philippines and is more fully developed, with better highways, transportation, hotels, and other facilities. Let's take a detailed look at this country.

The Kingdom of Thailand is located in Southeast Asia. It is bordered by Laos, Cambodia, Malaysia, and Myanmar (formerly Burma). Further to the north is China and to the east is the Philippines.

Known as Siam until 1938, Thailand is a constitutional monarchy under a parliamentary democracy system of government. Thus it is ruled by a king, who is largely a figurehead, with a governing body made up of three branches – the executive, the legislative and the judiciary. The present sovereign, King

Bhumibol Adulyadej, is the world's longest reigning monarch and is widely beloved by the Thais.

Thailand is a little less than 200,000 square miles in size with a population of approximately 64 million. The climate is tropical, with a rainy season that starts in May and runs through October.

About 95% of the people are Buddhist and most of the rest are Muslim. Many tourists come to Thailand to visit the Buddhist temples, while others come to visit the bar girls. I did not come to visit either, preferring to indulge in my enjoyment of fine beaches and equally fine female companions.

I'm also a scuba diver and I found that the diving was pretty good but the marine life was not as varied as I had expected, probably because of the tsunami that had occurred shortly before I began my visits.

Travel Requirements

A visa is not required for stays of 30 days or less. However, your passport must be valid for at least six months from your date of entry. If you expect to stay more than 30 days you can purchase a 60-day tourist visa from a Thai embassy in the US. You can either go in person or send your passport, along with two passport-type photos and the required fee. You must also include a prepaid return envelope. I strongly suggest using a reliable courier service such as FedEx or UPS.

If you overstay, you will be fined on a per-day basis when you depart. An alternative is to cross into a neighboring foreign country, such as Laos, Vietnam, or Cambodia. Your return to Thailand, even on the same day, will be treated as a new entry and will allow you to stay for another 30 days.

Flying to Thailand

Bangkok, the capital of Thailand and major port of entry, is 8623 air miles from Los Angeles. Flight time via Thai Airways, the only airline flying there non-stop, is 17 hours and 20 minutes, and the return flight is 16 hours and 5 minutes (the difference being due to a prevailing jetstream of westerly winds). For other airlines requiring a change of planes along the way, add 1-3 hours or more of travel time.

Although I have flown to Thailand 16 times I have never booked on Thai Airways because their fare is usually several hundred dollars more than whatever other airline happens to be cheapest at the moment. I don't mind changing planes if I can save that kind of money and if the departure and arrival times are convenient.

My favorite choice for Thailand is EVA, a Taiwanese airline. Their fares are usually among the lowest, the aircraft are clean, the service is friendly and efficient, and the meals are pretty good for airline food. What's more, you have your own entertainment screen with a choice of movies that start when you want them to. Many airlines, particularly the US carriers, have one screen per cabin area and you watch whatever happens to be on.

EVA offers a choice of economy fares, the higher ones giving you various change or cancellation options. An Economy Plus upgrade (also called Elite) gives you roomier seating and better food. When you book online you can make your seat selection from a seating diagram of the airplane, so you can see where you'll be in relation to the galley, restrooms, etc. Also, an online check-in function, available 24 hours before departure, puts you on a fast track at the airport check-in counter.

Almost all international flights arrive at the fairly new Suvarnabhumi (pronounced soo-var-nuh-BOOM) Airport in

Bangkok. However, you can also fly direct from some US cities to two popular tourist destinations, Phuket and Chiang Mai.

Travel within Thailand

Most flights from Bangkok to other Thai cities originate from the older Don Mueang Airport, but a few domestic airlines use the newer international Suvarnabhumi Airport, so you really need to be sure which is the right airport for your flight. Thai Air is the major carrier. Among the budget domestic airlines are Nok Air (owned by Thai Air), AirAsia, and One Two Go. Flights to many popular destinations take about an hour from Bangkok and cost about $60-110, depending on the airline. You can book online.

You can also travel domestically via buses and trains. I have not ridden on a Thai train, but I get the impression that buses are the preferred mode of public transportation. There are two types of buses – the standard bus, which is not air conditioned and can be a vintage vehicle, and the VIP bus, which is air-conditioned and has comfortable reclining seats.

Bus travel is cheap. For example, I took a VIP bus from Khon Kaen to Udon Thani, a trip of 70 miles. The fare was about $3 and there was a hostess on board who served free snacks!

How you get about within a city depends on what city you're in. Bangkok has a monorail system called the Skytrain, as well as metered taxis and tuk-tuks. A tuk-tuk (pronounced "took-took") is basically a long-bodied motorcycle with three wheels and a passenger compartment that seats up to three people. It is noisy, cheap, and the trip is often hair-raising. Before getting in, negotiate a price with the driver. No need to tip him.

The taxi drivers are fairly honest, but will often try to charge you a flat rate. Insist on their using the meter – it will always be cheaper. Tipping is customary.

Most Thai cities do not have taxis. Public transportation is by tuk-tuk or songthaew – a small bus in the form of a pickup truck with a passenger compartment seating up to eight people. For personal transportation, motorcycles and scooters far outnumber cars, and it is not unusual to see a family of four crowded onto a two-wheeler, with mom holding an open umbrella as a shield from the hot sun.

You can rent a scooter for $7.50 to $9.00 for a day, less by the week or month. Rental cars, where available, are priced about the same as in the USA. (They are actually called "hired cars" in Thailand, whereas "rental cars" are supplied with drivers.)

Two things to keep in mind: (1) Driving is on the *left* side of the road. (2) Safety procedures are generally disregarded, with vehicles zooming heedlessly out of side streets and cutting in and out with abandon. This requires special caution when you are on foot, as vehicles will always assume the right of way.

Food

You can eat well at low cost in Thailand, provided you eat Thai food – not really a hardship, as Thai cuisine is world-renowned, and even a sidewalk food stall might surprise you with a good, albeit simple, meal.

In the average restaurant, a large bowl of coconut milk soup or spicy seafood soup with a generous mound of rice will cost about $4.50. Many other dishes are priced about the same – shrimp, fish, chicken or beef, prepared in a variety of ways. American and European dishes, as well as fancier Thai specialties, will run $9-18.

Thai Massage

Thailand is famous for massage. As Thailand is equally famous for its sex trade, you might suspect that if you entered a massage parlor, sex would be readily available. No doubt this is true in many parlors, but all I ever asked for was a massage, and I was always happy with the result.

Thai massages are very good and very cheap. A one-hour massage costs about $9 (plus tip) except in a hotel, where you can expect to pay more. Massage parlors abound in big cities and resorts.

If you choose a foot massage you are seated in a comfortable chair. If you want a body massage you are ushered into an area that has a cushioned mat and curtains all around for privacy. You strip down to your underwear and are given a gown to wear. The massage is provided by a female, often young and attractive and usually very friendly.

It is a pleasant experience and very invigorating. Massagers also ply their trade on many beaches.

If you are taking a Thai girl out, she will almost certainly enjoy a massage on an adjoining mat.

Hotels and Resorts

This is not a travel guidebook, but there are a few places I can personally recommend. Note that the rates I quote should be used as general guidelines. They might be considerably different according to season and whether the rooms are booked through the hotel or an online travel agent.

Bangkok. This is where the US Embassy is, so it's where you'll be if you accompany your girl for the visa interview process. I stayed at the Oakwood City Residence (one of several Oakwood facilities there). A suite, with living room, bedroom, and kitchenette costs about $90, including breakfast. I don't recall if it was close to the embassy, as I was being chauffeured by my attorney, but I remember it as being very nice, with a beautiful pool.

Another favorite of mine is the President Park, which has similar suite accommodations, also at $90 with breakfast. A supermarket is within walking distance and there is a free shuttle service to a shopping mall.

If you want a good central location, consider the Holiday Inn Silom, within walking distance of shopping – including a night market (endless booths at which low-priced clothing, shoes, and other items are sold into the wee hours) and a variety of restaurants. Rooms start at $90, including a very good breakfast.

If you have a connecting flight the next day and want a hotel near one of the airports, here are some choices. The Airport Novotel is situated right at Suvarnabhumi. This convenience comes at a fairly high price, the lowest Internet rate being $146, which does not allow you to cancel or even change dates, and does not include breakfast. An unusual policy allows you to choose your own check-in time and then check out 24 hours later.

About a ten-minute taxi ride from Suvarnabhumi is the rather unique 13 Coins Airport Grand, with park-like grounds that include a small artificial lake, rope swings, a small swimming pool, and other outdoor amenities. There are two types of rooms: modest, at $45, and tremendous (including a table that seats about a dozen people!) at $90. A somewhat limited sit-down breakfast is included. The indoor-outdoor restaurant has a large menu and nightly musical entertainment with some customer participation. (I sang there during all of my stays.) There is free Internet service in the lobby.

I could go on and on about this place and its interesting Chinese proprietor, but that's almost a book in itself.

If your connecting flight leaves from Don Mueang Airport, I recommend the nearby Miracle Grand Convention Hotel. Room rates start at $55, including breakfast, and Wi-Fi is free. Its main dining room is called the Coffee Shop, but the name is misleading, as the restaurant serves a fine buffet in nice surroundings. There is also a Chinese restaurant on the mezzanine.

Pattaya. This beach resort is approximately two hours' drive from Bangkok. I don't much like it because the main beaches are crowded to the point where the bathers are packed sardine-like into deck chairs several rows deep and the sea is not very clean.

There is a section of maybe a dozen blocks called the Night Walk, so named because it is closed at night to vehicular traffic but wide open to trafficking in ladies of the night, as well as former boys who have been surgically reconfigured for the purpose.

Within this area are the expected raunchy entertainment bars but also some good restaurants, including a classy outdoor buffet.

What made Pattaya worth visiting for me was a condo that I rented to please a female companion who hankered to spend some time there. I found the condo through a UK website called vacation-homes.com, which provides descriptions and photos of condos in many locations, plus available dates, costs, and links to the owners. This particular property was in a gated community mercifully distant from Pattaya's hurley-burley. It had two bedrooms, two bathrooms, a living room with dining area, a kitchen, and an enclosed patio with a small private swimming pool.

There was also a large community pool and a restaurant. The rental was $503 for 10 days. A beach was within walking distance, but it was badly littered. We did discover a beautiful resort on the beach, bearing the unlikely name of Cabbages & Condoms. (The owner is an avid promoter of birth control.)

Their restaurant looks out on the sea and serves excellent food. I had the pleasure of walking through the resort's forest-like grounds with its lush foliage, orchids and other flowers, and a peaceful stream, and I would seriously consider staying there sometime. Rates start at $80.

We were some distance from shopping and the main part of Pattaya so we rented a scooter for $7.50 a day and that took us to some cleaner beaches nearby. Our condo was in immaculate condition, but for the first three days there was no TV because the owner, who lived in the UK, had not paid the satellite bill.

Phuket. This is probably Thailand's most popular tourist area and – as you might have noticed – the place I visited most often. It is a large island, easily reached from Bangkok by air. The most populous part is Patong, which I generally avoided due to its overcrowding and the aggressive vendors who roam the beach pushing everything from souvenirs to time-share condos.

Also on the scene are lots of bars that are well-decorated by, of course, bar girls. (I once saw an online promotion by a bar that offered to meet your flight with a limo that was well-stocked – actually, well-*stacked* – with two of its girls, whom you could pre-select on their website. This airport pickup, so to speak, sounded ideal for Type A personalities who just couldn't wait to dive in.)

If you prefer a quieter environment, Kata Beach and the more distant Karon Beach are more suitable.

The hotel I stayed at most often was the Kata Poolside because it is relatively inexpensive and the accommodations are very nice. The immaculate rooms are fairly large, with a balcony and a bathroom that includes a bathtub and separate stall shower.

The pool is sizable and the walk to the beach is only two blocks. The included buffet breakfast is just okay. Depending on the season and length of stay, the rate is $35-$80 a day.

A charming boutique hotel is the Kata Delight, overlooking the sea from its hillside perch. You can enjoy the view from your room and while paddling about in their infinity pool. Rates for a Deluxe room, including a good sit-down breakfast, start at $90.

Kata's Seven Mile Beach is clean and well-populated but not overcrowded and the vendors who walk the beach selling food, clothing, and trinkets are not pushy. Scuba dive operators run day trips to the outlying islands.

For a deluxe holiday, Phuket has a Club Med. A week for two persons in this all-inclusive resort will set you back $2100 or more. I have not stayed at this particular resort but I have been to three other Club Meds and found the food, facilities, and entertainment very good. The minimum-priced rooms were ordinary, but one doesn't spend much time in the room at a Club Med.

Koh Samet. This island, reached by ferry, is much smaller and quieter than Phuket. I have stayed twice at the Sai Kaew Beach Resort. Based on a recent visit to their website, it would appear that their former very plain Standard rooms, which are close to the main beach, have been upgraded and are now quite pricey.

I stayed in one of the Deluxe rooms, currently priced at $115, breakfast included. Although these rooms are not large, they are charmingly decorated and are located near the swimming pool and a secluded section of beach. This is truly a romantic setting, enhanced by some nearby restaurants where you can dine right on the sand, sitting on a mat and enjoying fresh seafood at a low candle-lit table a few yards from the sea.

Koh Chang. This is another small island, also reached by ferry. I stayed at a very nice place, Bhumiyama Beach Resort, adjoining a quiet section of white sand beach. My Deluxe room, priced at $826 for seven nights, breakfast included, was not large, but featured an outdoor bathroom complete with a rock-adorned bathtub – very atmospheric.

There is a nice pool and the food is good. A village is within walking distance, but there's not much to do except enjoy the beach and a female companion, which is always fine with me.

Hua Hin. This bustling town features a white sand beach that's densely packed with sun lounges, and you might prefer to rent or buy a mat and find a secluded spot under a tree. Horseback riding is available along the shore.

I rented a condo about a half-hour scooter ride away, again through vacation-homes.com. It had three bedrooms, two bathrooms, a living room, dining area, kitchen, and a small private swimming pool. The rental was $452 for seven days and the owner gave us an eighth day free.

Chiang Mai. Popular with tourists, Chiang Mai is in the northern part of Thailand. I stayed at the Park Hotel, a short tuk-tuk ride from the main part of the city and reasonably priced at about $35. Their restaurant is good and there are also two nice Japanese restaurants – one across the street and the other a short walk away.

You can opt for a one-hour elephant ride in one of several elephant parks. The guide will stop at some point, dismount, and he'll use your camera to take photos of you aboard the elephant.

In the morning, the pachyderms put on a show, playing soccer and imitating humans in other ways. My favorite: five elephants, each seated at an easel with a paint brush in its trunk, and each creating a painting in an individual artistic style. (You just can't beat Thailand for culture.)

Near Chiang Mai is **Chiang Rai**, where the hill tribes live and put on their native dances for groups of tourists.

Udon Thani. This city has nothing much to recommend it except for girl-hunting, but that's good enough, as a substantial number of attractive ThaiLoveLinks members live in that area. As I have mentioned earlier, I stayed each time in the Charoensri Grand Royal hotel – a nice place with a good restaurant (especially the buffet lunch, including all-you-can-eat sashimi), conveniently located one block from a Robinsons mall and a large variety of restaurants. Rooms are priced at $40.

Khon Kaen. This place is even less interesting than Udon Thani, but you might find yourself visiting there, as I did, to meet some ThaiLoveLinks girls. I stayed at the Charoen Thani Princess, an old but pleasant hotel. Recently, I read some guest complaints that the rooms were somewhat worn-out, but the two times I was there in 2008-2009 I found the furnishings attractive and comfortable. The rooms are priced at $40.

Ubolrat. This is a picturesque area about an hour's drive from Khon Kaen. I spent a week there, wife-hunting, and remember it often with pleasure. Adjoining a large and scenic park is a huge lake (actually a dam) that stretches as far as the eye can see. Sightseeing trips on small pontoon boats are available. Overlooking the lake is a very good restaurant.

There are a couple of other restaurants in town, plus numerous roadside food stands. I stayed at a small resort called Reaun Arraya. The staff were very friendly. I occupied one of their two-room suites, small but comfortable and an excellent value at $17 a day. There was a large pool and a small restaurant with a limited menu. Thai massages could be had on their premises at reasonable cost.

In the next chapter we'll visit the Philippines.

12

GIRL-HUNTING IN THE PHILIPPINES

The Philippines consists of about 7000 islands in the Western Pacific. It was a Spanish colony from 1556 to 1898. The Spaniards brought in missionaries to convert the Filipinos to Catholicism, and currently about 80% of the population is Catholic. The Catholic influence drives civil laws, which has special significance to you if you marry there. (See the chapter titled "Suppose it Doesn't Work Out?")

In 1898 the United States acquired control of the country by defeating Spain in the Spanish-American war. The Filipinos revolted against the Americans and subsequently established the Commonwealth of the Philippines in 1935. During WW II the country was occupied by the Japanese until they were driven out by American forces.

As a result of the American influence, schoolchildren are taught basic English as well as Tagalog, the national Philippine language. (Actually, there's a total of about 80 Philippine languages and dialects!) The Philippines became an independent republic in 1946. The country is governed by three branches – executive, legislative, and judicial.

Current population is approximately 94 million. The climate is tropical, with considerable rainfall from May to November. Typhoons occur periodically at all times of the year. I made five trips to several parts of the Philippines throughout 2010, visiting my wife while we waited out her visa application, and I felt that the weather there was more oppressive – hotter and rainier – than in Thailand. Also, Philippine food is not nearly as creative as Thai cuisine.

If I had to choose between the two countries to live in, or even visit, it would be a no-brainer: Thailand. I did find my wife in the Philippines, after thrashing about in Thailand for a long time, and perhaps that was a matter of luck. My advice to those starting the hunt is to check the matchmaking websites for both countries and see what lights your fire.

Travel Requirements

A visa is not required for stays of up to 21 days. (Note that this is nine days less than the time allowed in Thailand.) Your passport must be valid for at least six months from the date of your arrival. Also, the immigration form you present on arrival (the form will be given to you during your flight) must include a date and flight number for your departure.

You can obtain a visa for longer periods ranging from three months to one year by purchasing it from a Philippine Embassy in the US or by applying for an extension at a Bureau of Immigration office in the Philippines.

Flying to the Philippines

Manila, the capital of the Philippines, is 7295 air miles from Los Angeles. I use Philippine Airlines (PAL), which flies direct to Manila at reasonable cost. Flight time is 16 hours 30 minutes LAX-MNL and the return flight is 13 hours 5 minutes. (On the LAX-MNL flights, the westerly headwinds usually necessitate a brief refueling stop in Hawaii or Guam). You can also fly direct from some US airports to the Philippine city of Cebu.

If you are continuing from Manila to another city in the Philippines, it's generally best to get ticketed on PAL all the way to your final destination rather than purchasing separate flights – especially if you want to check more than one piece of baggage.

For example, suppose you want to fly from LAX to Manila and then continue on to Tacloban. If you get ticketed all the way through (LAX-MNL-TAC) you can check two pieces of baggage all the way to Tacloban at no extra charge. However, if you buy a ticket from LAX to MNL and a separate ticket from MNL to TAC, you will be restricted to one free piece of checked baggage for MNL-TAC and you will be assessed a high surcharge for each extra bag. In addition, once you arrive in Manila you'll have to haul your checked baggage from the International terminal to the domestic terminal.

Travel within the Philippines

The major airlines providing domestic transportation are Philippine Airlines and Cebu Pacific. Other airlines include Air Asia Philippines, AirPhil Express, Asia Pacific, and SEAIR. The lowest economy fares (which are not really very low) are not refundable and the penalties for making any changes are so rapacious that when I had to change the departure date for a PAL flight from Manila to Tacloban for me and my wife, it was actually cheaper to throw out the round trip tickets, costing about $185, and start all over again. (All of this and more was made necessary by the US Embassy, which moved up my wife's visa interview on short notice.)

Inter-city buses in the Philippines are often non-scheduled, operating only when they have a full load, with passengers stoically waiting at a bus stop for an hour or so, then possibly standing for several hours in the bus that finally arrives. During some holidays the buses don't run at all!

However, there is fairly good public transportation within the cities, much of it provided by jeepneys. These are buses that look as if they came out of a Disney movie, decorated with wild paint schemes and lots of chrome. They are almost always full, sometimes with passengers hanging out the back.

For short trips you can take a pedicab, a bicycle-powered taxi with a sidecar carrying one or two passengers. The fare in some cities is a modest 5 pesos (about 11 cents) per passenger.

You can rent a motorcycle for about $9 for a day, with discounts for longer periods. Rental cars, where available, are priced about the same as in the USA. Driving is even more eye-widening in the Philippines than in Thailand because most of the roads have only two lanes even on long inter-city routes, adding to the number of times a vehicle will be passing another and coming at you head-on. With that notable exception, traffic in the Philippines moves on the familiar right-hand side.

As a pedestrian, you have the same rights in the Philippines as in Thailand – that is, vehicles always have the right of way because they're made of metal and you're not.

Hotels and Resorts

As I mentioned in the previous chapter, this is not a travel guidebook, but here are a few places I have stayed at and can recommend:

Manila. This crowded, rather dingy metropolis is the Philippines' capital city and airport of entry. It is also the location of the US Embassy, so you'll have to spend some time there if you are bringing your fiancée or wife home. (Much more on that in the chapter titled "Getting Her Here.")

The embassy is in the Ermita section, and the nearby hotel I found to be acceptable is the Paragon Tower. It is within walking distance of both the embassy and the St. Luke's Medical Extension, where your gal will have to get her medical exam prior to the interview.

The hotel has spacious, clean rooms and bathrooms, some with bathtubs, and plenty of hot water (not always found in Asian hotels). There is free Wi-Fi in the lobby and a free, albeit mediocre, breakfast. Rooms are priced at $56-65.

I visited the nearby Ralph Anthony Suites, which have nicely furnished suites that include kitchenettes, starting at $50. I would have rented one but they were full up at the time. Some other hotels in the area are priced as low as $33, but not all provide free Internet and breakfast.

Also in Ermita is a gigantic Robinsons mall. You can literally lose yourself on the three floors that fan out in all directions, packed with mostly upscale shops and a wide variety of restaurants that are better than any I encountered elsewhere in the area. Tip: For relatively low-priced goods, search out the arcade on the main floor.

Tacloban. This is another one of those rather nondescript cities that you would probably not bother to visit unless you were meeting a girl there. The Leyte Park Resort Hotel consists of a main building and a group of villas fronting the San Pedro Bay.

The hotel was built in 1979 by Imelda Marcos, widow of the notorious president Ferdinand Marcos. If you book a room, ask for accommodations that have been renovated; you'll pay a little more, but the difference will be worth it. Rates for renovated rooms start at $48 if you make a reservation. Oddly, if you walk in without a reservation you will pay *less*. I discovered this on checking in, and since I was going to stay for 10 days, the walk-in saving was substantial, but no, I was told, I had made a reservation and of course would have to pay the higher rate.

They didn't have my money yet, so I said, "Fine – I will pay the reservation rate for tonight, then tomorrow we will check out, walk out the door, turn around, walk back in and book a room for the lower rate." The clerk looked puzzled by this logic, then summoned a manager, who also pondered the situation. Finally I was assured I would be billed at the lower rate – after the first night.

Also available are what they call *apartelles* that have an electric burner for cooking, at $170 a week plus your usage of electricity and water.

Hotel amenities include an adult pool and a children's pool, plus three pretty good restaurants.

I obtained for Fely a furnished apartment in Palo, a town adjacent to Tacloban, and this gave us much-needed privacy during the long wait for her visa. The rent was about $220 a month, plus utilities that added another $100 or so. (Yes, power is expensive in the Philippines, especially with air-conditioning.)

It was a bungalow, with a sizable living room, two bedrooms, two bathrooms, and a kitchen. We had to provide our own linens and kitchenware, and do our own cleaning. We saw other apartments in the area for as little as $110 a month – some unfurnished and some without air-conditioning or hot water for showers.

A historical feature of Palo is the MacArthur Landing Memorial, with statues depicting Gen. Douglas MacArthur and soldiers wading ashore in Leyte during WW II.

Tahusan Beach. This is promoted as the best beach in southern Leyte province. Uh-huh. We stayed for several days at the Dona Marta, a boutique resort. We had one of their two small-but-pleasant rooms facing the Pacific Ocean. The rate was $50 a night, which included breakfast. We took our other meals in the only restaurant within walking distance. Considering that we were often their only customers (with good reason), the wait for their just-okay food was exasperating.

The beach itself, while clean, was coarse brown sand with some small rocks underfoot in the water. (I understand that the nearby islands of St. Paul and St. Peter have very nice white sand beaches.) The hotel had no pool but it had a Jacuzzi – well, sort of. As we were also the hotel's only customers, the manager refused to spend money to heat the water. This cooled us off to the extent that we left sooner than we had planned. Fely still has fond memories of the place because it was quiet and rather nice despite its drawbacks.

Negros Oriental. For a month-long visit with Fely I rented a bungalow (through islandsproperties.com) in a resort called Dumaguete Springs. The cost was $1000 for the month. The bungalow had a nice little kitchenette and the resort itself was located on a beach. However, the beach was not that great – here again, the sand was brown and also had a muddy consistency, but there was a nice pool. Daily maid service was provided. I was able to rent a motorcycle for the month for $135. We did our shopping in the Robinsons Mall in Dumaguete.

The past two chapters gave you a taste of travel in Thailand and the Philippines. Now let's suppose you find the Asian girl of your dreams and the question comes up: Instead of bringing her to the USA, suppose you move to her country? The next chapter discusses that possibility.

13

MOVING TO HER COUNTRY

You might assume that the woman of your choice would want very much to move to the United States, but suppose she doesn't? Suppose she is perfectly comfortable in her own environment and is reluctant to relocate thousands of miles away from her family?

Would you consider pulling up stakes and moving to her country? Such a move would very likely have both upsides and downsides. There are books about working in or retiring to various countries and if you're seriously thinking of doing that you should read them, and, more important, travel to your country of choice and spend a lot of time there before committing yourself. Meanwhile, I'll offer a few observations.

On the plus side ...

The Living is
Somewhat Cheaper

Yes, the once-almighty dollar is still worth quite a lot in some Asian countries, although at this writing the dollar has become steadily weaker, having lost about 10 percent of its value against both the Thai baht and the Philippine peso in about three years' time.

Housing is much cheaper than comparable US accommodations. However, I have found, somewhat to my disappointment, that my grocery bills in the Asian supermarkets were about as high as they are in my home state of California, which is not famous for low prices.

True, I was able to save money by shopping for produce in the outdoor markets, but I drew the line at buying meat and seafood that had been lying on counters in the heat, touched by customers and flies alike.

Clothing, housewares, and other day-to-day items are not any cheaper overseas, and such items as computers and cameras are considerably *more* expensive. Motorcycles and cars, which do not have to meet US safety standards, are cheaper.

All-in-all, I have seen reports by expats who state that a couple can maintain a simple existence (food, modest shelter, utilities) for as little as $600 a month and live on a fairly grand scale for $2000. One benefit is the availability of cheap labor for household and other help.

She Might be Happier

If she doesn't want to move to the USA, it's almost a sure thing she wants to stay near her family. Of course, as a compromise you could offer to send her back for a visit once or twice a year if you can afford it.

Also, she might have concerns about being an alien in a strange land, especially if you don't live near a community of people from her country. I have some suggestions about that in the chapter titled "Keeping Her Spirits Up."

You Might Like It Better, Too

Americans and other foreigners who relocate to Thailand or the Philippines report that they are delighted with the more relaxed lifestyle and neighborliness they have found, as well as the lower cost of maintaining a good lifestyle.

On the minus side ...

Foreigners Receive Second-Class Treatment

In the USA, foreigners who are here legally (and some who are not) have the same ability as American citizens to own property and businesses. As a foreigner in Thailand and the Philippines, you can own a house, but not the land on which it sits. (Put it in your wife's name and hope for the best.)

If you establish a business, you can have only a minority interest; controlling interest must be held by one or more nationals of that country. There are ways around this, but they could be risky.

You must get your visa renewed periodically. And it is widely said (although I have no proof) that in a legal dispute between you and a national, the cards are often stacked against you.

Suppose You Get Sick?

Medical facilities in these countries do not compare with those in the USA. Your existing health insurance might not cover you in a foreign country; Medicare certainly doesn't. However, health insurance abroad is available and medical treatment is much cheaper.

As an extreme example, once I was with a lady companion in the Thai resort area of Phuket. She developed an upset stomach and wanted to go to a hospital. We were directed to a small clinic. Its reception area was open to the street, like a bar or restaurant. My lady and I waited for a short while on a bench, after which she was sent to a room where she consulted with the doctor. He gave her a prescription, which we took to the dispensary in the reception area and there she received three envelopes containing different pills. The cost of the medical consultation and the pills totaled 66 baht, or a little over $2.

Probably more realistically for a foreigner (but still very cheap) are some costs I've read about from an expat in the Philippines: An office visit to a doctor, $8.50; a chest x-ray, $7.00; a stay in a hospital, $53 per day for the room plus medicine and lab charges.

In Thailand, a pharmacist can sell you a prescription medicine simply by writing the prescription, which can save you a visit to the doctor if you have confidence in the pharmacist. Philippine law requires that a prescription be written by a doctor, same as here.

On the questionable side ...

Will You be Happy in a Different Culture?

You might have to modify your behavior to fit the customs of your adopted country. You will undoubtedly find it more convenient and more socially acceptable if you learn the language.

You will probably have to accustom yourself to different sanitation standards. For example, even in large cities there are relatively few supermarkets where perishables are kept under refrigeration. Trash cans do not abound and the street is handy for garbage disposal. I do not mention this to disparage the inhabitants; they live in poor countries and make do with what they have.

Many foreigners stay comfortably within their culture by living in or near an expat community and forming friendships with like-minded Westerners. Others get fully integrated with the people of their host country, learn their language, and adapt to their customs. As with much of life, it's best to gravitate to what makes you happy.

Unrest Happens

From time to time you'll see political instability in either country. For example, a few years ago Thailand was rocked by demonstrations and counter-demonstrations, centering largely around a prime minister who was accused of corruption and ousted by a military coup. Rioting crowds, allegedly purchased by the ex-official, occupied the country's major international airport and various government buildings.

But this was relatively benign when compared to incidents in the Philippines – particularly Mindanao and other southern portions, where tourists have been kidnapped and held for ransom. A particularly heinous event took place in 2009, when scores of people were brutally massacred. Most of them were Filipinos and their families, but foreign reporters were also slain.

I became immediately aware of the permanent state of alert when I arrived in Manila and checked into a hotel. I got into the elevator and found that it was being operated by a uniformed security guard with a large revolver strapped to his waist. Not your everyday bellhop! The next day I saw more of these guards in office buildings and even fast food restaurants and small shops. On entering a shopping mall, I passed through a security checkpoint manned by a guard with a metal-detector wand. I later discovered that this is commonplace in Philippine shopping malls.

I flew to Davao, in the southern part, to meet my future wife. She cautioned me against going out without having her along "for protection." (She is 4'11" and weighs 100 pounds.)

One way to get more insight on living in the Philippines as an expat is by joining the mailing list MAG-ANAK@yahoogroups.com. (MAG-ANAK means "family" in the Philippine language of Tagalog.) Websites of some other groups are listed in the Appendix.

A large number of MAG-ANAK members have moved to the Philippines and seem to be quite happy with their decision.

Regardless, I strongly suggest that before you get too serious about an Asian girl, try to determine her true feelings about "my place or your place" and make sure you're both on the same page.

14

GETTING HER HERE

Finding the right girl is only half the battle. Getting her here to the United States is the other half (unless, of course, you decide to move to her country). You and she will have to persuade the US Government that the two of you are really in love and are planning to have a sincere, happy, forever-type marriage.

Why are the Feds putting their nose into your personal business? Well, one answer can be found in that infamous line, "We're from the Government and we're here to help." Yes, the Government is delving into your love life for your own good, so you need to be grateful. After all, the girl you've chosen might be taking advantage of you – pretending to love you in order to get to the USA, after which she will ditch you, and you wouldn't like that, would you?

If you think you're enough of a grownup to make those decisions for yourself, there is the alternate argument that the Government is protecting the girl from you, in case you plan to put her on the street as a prostitute.

Sure, some precautions are necessary to help prevent abuses. But what some people – this writer included – see as a problem is the over-zealousness that invariably takes place when anonymous bureaucrats are given virtually unlimited power and no accountability. Be that as it may, it's what you will have to deal with in order to get that precious visa for your lady.

I mention all this, not to discourage you, but to emphasize the importance of taking all the necessary steps – some of them logical, some of them not – to convince the all-powerful bureaucrats that you and your lady have the intention and the resources to get married and stay married.

What You Must Do

You, as petitioner (or a professional representing you) will complete the necessary forms on behalf of the beneficiary (your fiancée or spouse). The paperwork, along with a fee payment – at this writing, $340 for a fiancée visa and $420 for a spousal visa – is sent by a courier service to the USCIS (United States Customs and Immigration Service) office that serves your area. (More fees will come later.)

After a few weeks you will receive a Receipt Notice, which will include an identification number that has been assigned to your fiancée or wife. This number – usually preceded by "WAC" or "EAC" – will follow your lady throughout the process.

Keep the notice in a safe place, along with a copy of your application and all future paperwork. The USCIS has been known to lose an applicant's entire file, although they won't admit it. They will simply say "No record," implying that you never sent them anything. This happened to me once, but I was able to produce a FedEx notice of delivery, complete with the name of the staffer who had signed for it, and *voila!* the file was found. So be sure to send all materials via FedEx (my preference) or some other courier service that records all the delivery details.

You can periodically check your application's progress at uscis.gov and you can also sign up to receive automatic email updates if the status of your case changes

At some point you will need to file an Affidavit of Support – Form I-134 for a fiancée visa or Form I-864 for a spousal visa. You will list your income, bank accounts, stocks, bonds, real estate and other assets, to show that you are financially able to support your fiancée or wife.

The Affidavit of Support is a legal contract between you and the US Government and by signing it you acknowledge that you will be financially responsible if she becomes a public charge.

Proving the Seriousness of Your Relationship

How do you demonstrate that you and your lady have a bona fide relationship? First of all, the two of you must have met and spent time together before you file the application. You must collect proof in the form of photos of the two of you together – the more, the better.

I submitted 35 photos for our application and another 15 for the interview, or 50 in all. (One immigration attorney recommends a total of 100!) Why so many photos? In my dealings with the immigration authorities, I was often reminded of the question in a beer commercial: "Why ask why?" Just do it. True, it's unlikely that you and your lady will be in 50 different places, but you can shamelessly pad your evidence with, for example, various poses outside a hotel, other poses in the hotel lobby, more poses in the hotel restaurant, and more yet in your room.

Follow the same procedure in other locations. Make sure your faces are clearly recognizable – in good focus and without sunglasses or floppy hats. Use a camera with a date stamp and an automatic timer function for picture-taking when the two of you are alone.

Some romantic pictures are fine, but don't go beyond hugging and kissing. If you visit her family, include them in some shots, and it will be helpful if they are smiling. Also, provide copies of airline tickets and hotel receipts, as well as copies of your letters, emails, instant messages, and/or long distance phone bills – in short, everything that paints a picture of two people who are in love and have every intention of spending the rest of their lives together.

Remember, in the eyes of the immigration authorities, you and your foreign fiancée or wife start off under suspicion of creating a sham relationship in order to get her to the USA and you must prove otherwise.

Warning: You might be tempted to bypass these complications by having your girl apply for a tourist visa or student visa, but this could be a serious mistake if she does not meet the rigid qualifications. Her attempt to get here by one of those methods will be a matter of record, and your subsequent application for a fiancée or spousal visa could be denied on the basis of attempted fraud. (More on this in the next chapter.)

The Process

You will be applying for a K1 fiancée visa or, if you have already married her, a CR1, IR1, or the rather outmoded K3 spousal visa. I'll explain the differences shortly.

If your application is approved, it will be forwarded to the National Visa Center for further processing. If the NVC is satisfied with the application, the paperwork will be sent to the US embassy in your girl's country – for example, Bangkok if she's a Thai and Manila if she's a Filipina.

Eventually, your lady will be notified of her interview date. She must provide additional paperwork, including a police report certifying that she has no criminal record, and she must undergo a medical exam at an approved facility.

The interview is most important, for it is the interviewer who will decide whether or not to approve the application and issue the visa. Therefore, it is essential for your intended to make a favorable impression. I will provide some tips later on.

I also recommend that you attend the interview with her, not only to provide moral support, but also to give the interviewer the picture of a loving and committed couple, and to answer any questions that might relate to you. I realize that your trip overseas will be expensive and time-consuming, but the interview is where everything you've worked for will succeed or fail and this is the time to go that extra mile – or, in this case, several thousand miles.

If the application is approved, the visa will be embossed into her passport and it will be made available sometime within ten days or so. She will receive her paperwork in a sealed package, from which she can remove only her passport. The rest of the package is to be opened by an immigration officer at the US airport of entry.

Now here are details that will help you decide which type of visa best meets your needs.

The K1 Fiancée Visa

The K1 visa allows you to bring your fiancée to the United States for 90 days. If the two of you marry within that period, she can remain in the USA and apply for an adjustment of status that will make her a permanent resident. If you do not marry within 90 days, she is required to return to her country of origin.

One obvious advantage of the K1 is that it gives you and your fiancée the opportunity to live together in your home environment before you make the marriage commitment.

Another benefit is that the processing time for the fiancée visa could be a few months shorter than the processing time for a spousal visa. One might assume that a couple that has already made the marriage commitment would be processed *faster* than a couple that hasn't, but you could go broke betting on USCIS logic.

As of this writing, processing times for the fiancée visa can run anywhere from four to seven months from the time of filing to the issuance of the visa. The schedules for all visas are subject to change. For current processing times and considerable other information visit uscis.gov.

The fiancée visa is probably the best option for most couples. However, there might be circumstances under which it is desirable or necessary to marry your lady in her country. For example, she or her parents might want the commitment of marriage before you whisk her to a strange land thousands of miles away. Or you could be ineligible for a K1 if, like the impulsive author of this book, you have already brought two foreign fiancées to these shores.

The limitation of two fiancée visas per customer is part of a 2005 Federal law called the International Marriage Broker Regulation Act, designed to curb abuses of "mail order brides." (A waiver of the limitation might be granted, but it's a gamble because you won't know for sure until you're well into the application process.)

If you marry overseas you apply for one of the following spousal visas:

The IR1, CR1, and K3

The IR1 is issued to those who have been married for two years or more at the time of the visa application. "IR" stands for Immediate Relative and the wife receives a green card that's valid for 10 years. The CR1 is issued to those who have been married for less than two years at the time of the visa application. "CR" stands for Conditional Resident and the wife receives a green card that's valid for two years.

Within 90 days of the green card's expiration date, she must file for a Removal of Conditions (Form I 751) and show that she still has a strong marriage with the husband who brought her here.

Supporting documentation should include affidavits from friends and/or relatives attesting to the relationship, copies of all income tax returns filed since the marriage, copies of driver's licenses or other government-issued photo IDs showing that she lives at your address, and, if applicable, joint bank accounts and joint ownership of property.

All of this stuff can be mailed in, but if the authorities have any serious questions they will feel perfectly free to call the both of you in for yet another interview. Once the application is approved, she will receive a ten-year green card. However, as the wife of a US citizen she can apply for citizenship after three years as a permanent resident.

The K3 is an option that is rapidly becoming obsolete. It was originally designed to reduce the visa processing time for spouses, keeping it more in line with the K1 fiancée visa. And, like the K1, the K3 does not automatically generate a green card, so your wife would have to apply for an adjustment of status upon her arrival in the USA. What's more, before you file a K3 application, you must have already filed an IR1 or CR1 application, which, when it is approved, will cancel the K3 application.

For the sake of brevity, I'm leaving out some details, but the bottom line is that it is a lot simpler to just file the IR1 or CR1 (whichever is applicable) and then you won't have to bother with the adjustment of status. My wife and I filed a CR1 and one week after she arrived in California she received her green card and social security card by Priority Mail.

There is also a DCF (Direct Consular Filing) available primarily if the US citizen and his foreign spouse are both permanently living abroad. Although the usual paperwork has to be completed, it can be filed directly with a foreign-based US embassy, thus avoiding the initial processing time in the USA. However, each embassy determines whether or not it will accept a DCF.

You Will Probably Need Help

It might seem pretty straightforward: Follow the instructions, fill out the forms, pay the fees. And maybe you can do it successfully on your own. Nevertheless, I advise you to strongly consider using the services of a competent professional who has seen what works and what doesn't work with the immigration and embassy people. Think of how much you have to lose if you slip up anywhere in process, causing the application to be considerably delayed – or worse yet, denied.

Search the Internet for fiancée or spousal visa services and you'll see a bunch of them, many using the high-pressure, boastful tones suggestive of an infomercial for a weight-loss program. Some of these services also start off with a low-ball fee of around $200, which turns out to be for simply filling out the forms, and then escalates to $600 or more to take you through the entire process. These are usually paralegal firms, meaning they are not lawyers. Immigration law firms charge upwards of $1500 to take you up to the embassy interview process, with an extra fee for adjustment of status if one is necessary.

The Help I Used

In the chapters that follow I provide details about my personal visa applications. For now, I will mention that over time I hired two lawyers and a paralegal for my various applications. The first lawyer was Michael Solomon, who practices in Nanuet, N.Y. I engaged Michael to process the K1 visa for my fiancée Nan and (to my ultimate regret, no fault of Michael's) the visa was granted.

Since that time Michael has enhanced his services with a support staff designed to give the fiancée or wife counseling by a native of her country. The staff includes a Filipina who was brought to the USA by her husband and now lives in New York City. There are staffers from other countries as well, but no one from Thailand as of now.

Michael's fees at this writing are as follows: K1 fiancée visa – $1295; adjustment of status (green card) – $1295; both of the above – $1995; CR1/IR1 – $1995.

Michael offers a money-back guarantee plus an extra $500 if his firm fails to get the visa, provided the client follows their directions and does not misrepresent any of the facts. His website is k-1-fiancée-visa-law.com

The lawyer I hired for three Thai marriage visa applications (mortifying details in a later chapter) was Brian Wright, an American immigration attorney who practices in Bangkok. Brian claims a 100% success rate in achieving visas, and offers a full refund if the application is denied due to his failure.

Brian strongly urges his clients to execute an optional prenuptial agreement (described in the chapter titled, "Suppose it Doesn't Work Out?"). It is worded in both Thai and English and includes the services of a Thai attorney to represent the fiancée.

Brian's current fees are as follows: K1 fiancée visa – $1695; adjustment of status (green card) – $1595; K3 spousal visa – $1995; CR1/IR1 – $2595; prenuptial agreement – $2950. Website : fianceevisathailand.com.

When I finally got it right by marrying Fely in the Philippines, I engaged a paralegal named Ray Bacon to handle the CR/1 application. I found Ray through the MAG-ANAK discussion group mentioned previously. Ray's office is in Sacramento, California. He charges a flat $400, which includes $120 for his assistant, Lucia, a Filipina located in Manila who prepares the women for their medical exam and crucial interview at the US Embassy.

I found both Ray and Lucia to be knowledgeable and conscientious – and certainly a great bargain compared to the fees charged by attorneys. Despite a seemingly minor paperwork omission that unleashed a Request for Evidence overkill by the NVC (described later), I do not hesitate to recommend Ray. He can be reached via multiethnicservices.com.

I will also mention an immigration attorney named Deron Smallcomb, who operates an office staffed with paralegals in San Diego, CA. I have not used his services, but he was highly recommended by Christian Filipina, a matchmaking service I referred to in the chapter titled "How to Meet Them."

I contacted Deron and he provided some information that appears in this chapter. He has two websites: EasyFiancéeVisa.com and EasyMarriageVisa.com. Fiancée visa services are available in three packages, ranging in price from $195 to $995. The spousal visa service is priced at $995 with optional native language support at an additional $300.

I repeat my urging to get professional help for the application process. Based on my own experience and some horror stories I have heard from others, I firmly believe it is too hazardous to try to sail through the procedure on your own, given that a mistake or omission could result in the application being delayed or denied. You don't want to risk that.

As to deciding between an immigration lawyer and a much-cheaper paralegal, hiring a lawyer who offers a money-back guarantee if the visa is denied might raise your comfort level to the point where the higher cost is acceptable. An important consideration is how quickly and thoroughly your representative will respond to inevitable questions that will come up during the process and you should try to get a feel for that before you make a commitment. For example, I found the paralegal Ray Bacon to be very prompt in responding to questions, whereas I often had to prod the lawyers I used.

Besides browsing the Internet, you might find some professionals in your area through a search engine or the yellow pages. Shop around, make sure you know what's covered in the quoted fees (government fees are *not* included) and try to get recommendations from satisfied clients.

There's More

If you want to bring a Filipina to the USA, she will have to go through some bureaucratic processes imposed by her own government. Following are the Philippine Government's instructions for obtaining the required permits:

As Filipinos going abroad as fiancé(e)s, spouses or other partners of foreign nationals, you are required to attend the guidance and counseling session of the CFO (Commission of Filipinos Overseas) in order to secure the Guidance and Counseling Certificate (GCC) and the CFO sticker. You need this certificate to renew or apply for a new passport at the Department of Foreign Affairs. You will also need to present this certificate together with your spouse/partner visa, at the Immigration office at the international airport on your day of departure.

To attend the seminar, you may proceed to either two of CFO's service providers: the St. Mary Euphrasia Foundation-Center for Overseas Workers (SMEF-COW) or the People's Reform Initiative for Social Mobilization, Inc. (PRISM).

You will have to bring with you the required documents to be accommodated in the counseling seminar. The counseling session runs for a minimum of two hours and is meant to provide you with adequate information regarding inter-marriage and migration, the cultural and social realities abroad as well as available support networks for women in distress, among others.

After you comply with all the requirements and finish the counseling session, you will be given the Certificate of Attendance, which you will have to bring along with other pertinent documents, to the CFO, for registration. Once you already have your valid passport and spouse/partner visa, then you have to register with the CFO. You will then be issued the GCC as well as the CFO Sticker.

In contrast to the Philippine government, the Thai government does not require any of the above procedures.

Later on I'll provide details on our own experiences with the visa process, including Fely's medical exam and our crucial interview at the US Embassy in Manila. But first I'll give you some tips on helping to keep your girl from feeling lonely when she gets here.

15

KEEPING HER SPIRITS UP

When you bring your lady to the United States, be aware that she might feel lonely – at least, at first. Sure, you'll be enveloping her with your love and consideration but there is a very good chance that she'll miss her family and friends at home. There are things you can do to make her feel better:

Community. Look for a community of people of her nationality. This is a bit of homework you can do before she comes to these shores. If she's religious, you'll probably want to find a congregation of her faith. If not, look for other organizations.

Using my home area as an example, I Googled "Filipino Community Organizations in Santa Barbara" and found one. There is also a nearby Catholic church that has a Saturday evening service conducted by a Filipino priest.

I did not find a Thai community organization but by scouting around I learned that there is a Thai Buddhist temple near my home and I attended a service. The congregation was made up mostly of Thai women and their American husbands.

Family connections. Encourage her to communicate regularly with her family. I have an international calling plan with my landline phone company, Verizon, which gives Fely 300 minutes of talk time a month for $10. And there are many international phone cards available on the Internet. Of course, webcam chats are even better if Internet service is available to her family.

Broadcasts from home. If she's a Filipina she can combat homesickness by enjoying movies and TV and radio programs that originate from the Philippines, free on her computer, by going to pinoy-ako.info. In fact, my wife sees the Filipino boxing idol Manny Pacquiao in live matches at no cost, while his same fights are sold to the rest of us at healthy prices on pay TV!

I'm not aware of any Thai version of that. However, you can get TV programs from Thailand and other nations by purchasing a ku band satellite receiver and a dish that's pointed at Galaxy 25. I found two companies, galaxy-marketing.com and sadoum.com, that sell complete systems starting at $159.

NAT TV provides Thai programming via a broadcasting station outside of Thailand. It's not clear where, but their website lists an address in North Hollywood, CA and they can be reached at info@nattv.com. Their home system sells for $279 and the website shows complete instructions for installing the dish.

I learned about these equipment providers by searching the web and I don't know anything about the quality of their systems.

More options. YouTube has clips of many foreign programs. Also, the music of your lady's country can be downloaded onto MP3 players and other devices.

Thai restaurants abound in many cities, largely because Americans have taken to the appetizing cuisine of that country. And although Filipino restaurants are quite scarce here, some foods imported from the Philippines can be found in Asian markets and online at such websites as philamfood.com, pinoyoutlet,com, and myfilipinogrocery.com.

If your gal's English is rudimentary, making it hard for her to communicate with your family and friends, you can offer to enroll her in an ESL (English as a second language) course at your local community college, where she'll meet others from her country. Alternatively, you can be her teacher with the help of a good grammar book and a multi-language dictionary.

If she had a scooter or motorcycle back home, consider buying one for her here, after she's become accustomed to our traffic laws and conditions.

In other words, do everything you can to make her feel that your country is also her country.

16

MY TWO FIANCÉE VISAS

I brought two fiancées to the USA – spaced about 10 years apart. The first was a young Chinese woman I'll call Mona.

Mona

I did not meet Mona on the Internet. I met her through her cousin Rosalyn, a friend I knew through ballroom dancing. Rosalyn knew I was single and one evening, during a break in the dancing, she asked me if I would be interested in her cousin Mona, who was living in China. I asked how old Mona was. "Twenty-four."

I was stunned. At the time, I was 72. I quickly did the math. That was an age difference of 48 years! Impossible! (My outlook on age differences would soon change radically.) While I was protesting, Rosalyn was fishing out an envelope, from which she handed me several photos of a cute, attractive girl. Next thing I knew I was asking for her address.

In those days, there was no e-mail or instant messaging, so we began a snail-mail courtship. It was soon followed by long-distance phone calls, which were then $1.25 a minute. After I got my first overseas phone bill I decided it was time to meet Mona in China.

During the flight, replete with the usual coughers and sneezers, I became infected with something and when Mona and her parents met me at the airport they encountered a frail-looking old man tottering weakly into the terminal.

Not my usual vibrant self and not, I felt, a good first impression. However, they were most gracious and welcoming. During my 10-day stay, they took me to three doctors. The second doctor threw out the medicine given to me by the first doctor and the third doctor likewise disposed of his predecessor's medication – an interesting aspect of time-honored Chinese healing.

Despite these medical excursions, the outcome of my visit was that Mona and I decided we had a future together and I returned home to arrange for her visa. That's when I made a bad mistake. Mona's cousin Rosalyn had gotten to these shores by means of a an American-sponsored student visa, for the purpose of enrolling in a California university. So I followed the same path by sponsoring Mona for a student visa, to avoid the time-consuming fiancée visa process.

What I didn't consider was that Rosalyn had an excellent scholastic record and had been offered a scholarship at the university. Mona had no such achievement and her application was denied. At that point we applied for the fiancée visa.

When it was time for her interview, Mona journeyed to the US Embassy in Guangzhou with her parents. (I had remained at home.) After the interview, Mona phoned me in tears to say she had been turned down by an official named West. I called the embassy and actually got through to him. (I doubt that you could do that these days.)

Mr. West explained that he denied her because she was obviously a liar who at first applied for the student visa and when that didn't work she applied for the fiancée visa. So he was protecting me, a gullible senior, from this wily young woman.

I didn't bother to explain that it had been *my* idea to apply for the student visa. Instead, I assured him that I had been introduced to Mona by a member of her family and I knew them to be very honorable, etc., etc. I continue to pitch him for what seemed like twenty minutes, expecting at any moment that he would hang up on me, but he didn't. Finally, he wearily said, "All right, tell her to come back tomorrow and I'll give her the visa."

Mona and I were married for six years, but the relationship was rocky and eventually terminated in a divorce. We remained friends and she re-married. Following the divorce, I threw myself onto the singles scene. I went to singles bars and dances and I joined a number of websites such as match.com, date.com, and AmericanSingles.com.

Not surprisingly, few American women of *any* age were interested in an 80-year-old man. I did meet some but there were no sparks on either side.

Then I decided to try Thailand because I had heard that the Thais were warm-hearted people and, as Asians, might not be bothered by large age differences. So I became a member of ThaiLoveLinks. Shortly after I joined, I was attracted to the photo and profile of a 25-year-old woman named Nan – and that *is* her real name. After several months of increasingly warm webcam chats I decided to meet her in her home town of Udon Thani, which was later to become a major hunting ground for me.

Nan

She met me at the airport, we went to my hotel room, and as soon as the door closed behind us her tongue was in my mouth. This struck me as being a very good start – perhaps *too* good a start if I had been using my head instead of another body part for guidance.

After a busy night, I met her parents, rice farmers, who greeted me warmly and seemed perfectly content to have me take their daughter away for a two-week holiday. Before I returned home I bought her an engagement ring.

Almost from the beginning there were various warning signs, which I noted, filed away, and tried to ignore. Several of them involved lies. For example, I phoned her once and she told me she was alone. When we concluded our conversation she forgot to turn off her cell phone and I heard her talking to a man. As the conversation was in Thai I didn't know what they were talking about and it might have been useful if I had. When I mentioned the incident later, she casually replied, "Oh, he was a friend of my father."

Despite noticing some other dubious statements I resolutely applied for her fiancée visa. When it was time for her interview I flew to Bangkok. Leaving no stone unturned, I obtained a letter from my Congresswoman, addressed to the official in charge of the embassy and expressing the hope that I would be given every consideration.

We sat in the embassy's large waiting room for several hours awaiting our turn. I watched as other applicants went up to the interview window and noticed that each examination took about 5 to 10 minutes. When we finally went to the window, the interviewer asked Nan, "How did you meet your fiancé?" "On the Internet," she replied. The official stamped a few papers and told us we could pick up her visa the next day. I have to assume that the Congresswoman's letter put us on a fast track.

Soon Nan was in my house in California. She stayed for a month, during which time she made considerable use of a laptop to chat with various friends. Investigation revealed that these new-found acquaintances were American guys who were being lined up to succeed me. Accordingly, I informed Nan that I had booked a flight for her to Thailand, since we were obviously not going to fulfill the visa's marriage requirement.

She took this calmly, agreed that she would be ready to depart the next morning, and went into the guest room to spend the night.

The next morning I entered the guest room to find that Nan had been replaced by a farewell note. I later learned that one of her new boyfriends, John, had driven down from northern California to help her out of the guest room window and into his car. John actually phoned me a few days later, offering to send me Nan's passport if she did not start behaving. I could hear Nan screaming at him in the background.

I wasted no time in driving down to the USCIS office in Los Angeles. There I presented a letter in which I described all that had taken place. Included in the letter were John's full name, phone number, and the city where he was harboring Nan in violation of the terms of her visa.

Barely stifling a yawn, the official told me that the Immigration "Service" would not go after Nan unless she committed a felony. Ah, my tax dollars at work!

The one piece of good news was that I had not married Nan. The not-so-good news was that the Affidavit of Support I'd signed as part of the visa application made me financially responsible for Nan for the next three years.

Fortunately for me, although not for him, John married Nan. Bizarrely, I continued to hear separately from both of them for many months afterward.

John followed in my footsteps in more ways than he had bargained for, discovering that she was still searching for other men. He eventually divorced her and my last words from Nan were complaints about *his* behavior and a disclosure that her next target was some guy in Las Vegas. If he was a gambler the odds were really against him this time.

In the next chapter I'll entertain you with accounts of even worse mistakes.

17

MY THREE THAI MARRIAGES

Yes, in this chapter I'm going to describe having married not one, not two, but three Thai women – and all within a two-year period! It's not a pretty picture and not easy for me to share with you. In fact, I debated long and hard with myself about whether to include this chapter in the book. Certainly, it does not enhance my image as an authority on anything, but my hope is that these revelations will serve as a warning not to act as impulsively – even once – as I did repeatedly.

As an explanation of sorts, I think these heedless plunges were motivated largely because I was in my eighties, the clock was ticking ever more loudly, and I wanted to get the lengthy visa process over with as quickly as possible. Of course, this haste, mindlessly repeated, was counter-productive. I set myself back by two years (not to mention thousands of dollars) and probably diminished myself in the eyes of the immigration authorities as a serial "marrier."

Anyway, here are the stories of those three Thai marriages.

Lin

I met Lin (I am not using real names here) through an introduction service located in the picturesque Thai town of Ubolrat. The business was run by a Thai named Sunimon and an expat from New Zealand named Jim. They had a website consisting of local girls, and they claimed, as such local services tend to do, that they investigated these girls before making them available to male members.

Most of those male members contacted the service from their homes in the US and other countries, and for a fee they were put in touch with the girls they were interested in. If a correspondence developed to where the man wanted to meet the girl, he would travel to Ubolrat.

The initial meeting with the girl would be chaperoned by the partners, who would also act as translators if necessary. All very respectable, and conducted in the romantic setting of a lakeside gazebo at a picturesque park.

I was already in Bangkok when I learned about the service. I called Jim and arranged transportation to Ubolrat. He and Sunimon got me settled at the Reaun Arraya resort (mentioned earlier) and then put me in front of a computer at their nearby office. I could choose as many girls as I wanted and the chaperoned meetings would take place for a fee of $50 each.

I chose six girls in all, arranging to meet the first three in one day, spaced apart so they would not encounter each other. The first one came to the park alone. She was quite nice, apologized for having gotten heavier since her photo had been taken, and promised to diet. She was also up front about having had a close relationship with a Finn who eventually threw her over. I put her in the "definitely consider" category and awaited the next visitor.

She arrived with a coterie of four girlfriends. I was not impressed with her, but I liked two of the girlfriends and I made this known to Jim after the meeting. However, it turned out that those girls were not interested in me.

Then Lin arrived with her mother. I was very impressed with her. For one thing, whereas the previous girls kept looking at the business owners when they were translating (most of them spoke some English but needed help to conduct a meaningful conversation), Lin never took her eyes from me. She really didn't have to, because her English was good.

Also in her favor was that she was quite stunning – tall and with a model's face and figure. During our meeting, Mom, who did not speak English, kept up a running conversation with Sunimon, and it turned out she was presenting her financial demands. The dowry would be 200,000 baht and I was assured that this was the Thai price – half the amount she would normally expect from a farang. (I later learned that Sunimon had privately arranged for a kickback of half of whatever I paid and therefore the dowry demand had been doubled so Mom could get the 100,000 she wanted.)

Over the next couple of days I met the remaining three – one of whom was a college student who brought along one of her teachers, I suppose to help her make an educated guess.

But I was fairly well hooked on Lin and the partners suggested that I rent a second room in the resort and invite Lin to stay there with Mom for a couple of days while we got to know each other better. The invitation was accepted and on the second day of their visit I took Lin to a scenic park and proposed to her. She accepted.

Sunimon told me I could take her on a trip "on approval," so to speak, following an engagement party in her village, provided I made a down payment on the dowry in the amount of 30,000 baht (about $1000). This was acceptable to me, so we had the engagement party at her house and then went to Phuket for a sort of prenuptial honeymoon.

I need not emphasize that an important aspect of what one might crudely call a test drive is what happens – or doesn't happen – in bed. Lin turned out to be what I have heard described as a *starfish* – that is, her concept of sexual intimacy was to assume a passive starfish-like position to accept whatever I wanted to do.

This was a start, but I was hoping for more enthusiastic participation as she got to know me. It never happened. Lin remained a starfish – at least with me.

But she was soooo beautiful, and that's what drove me to go ahead with the marriage. It was followed in short order by increasing indications of greed by both mother and daughter. I handled it as well as I could – giving in here, resisting there – and I felt it was something rather unpleasant I could cope with.

I returned home for a few months, sending monthly support payments plus the inevitable extras. However, the final blow came after my second visit to her. At her request, I rented a car and we toured around the countryside. When I came back home I discovered that $320 in traveler's checks were missing from my money pouch. This was glaringly evident, since I had not cashed any of the checks; I had used an ATM card for my expenses and carried the traveler's checks simply as a backup.

I called Lin and asked her about the checks. She denied taking them but the next day Mom called one of Sunimon's staffers, demanding to know how she could cash the checks. She was trying to deposit them into her account and, of course, the bank would not honor them.

This was crossing the line. I stopped sending support money, with the predictable result that Lin asked for a divorce. Under the circumstances, I was happy to oblige.

Nang

I met Nang through Willem, a German who had moved to the city of Udon Thani, married a Thai, and set up an introduction service. Willem and his wife made the familiar claim that they looked carefully into the backgrounds and reputations of the girls they represented. Supposedly a girl would pay Willem his fee when she became engaged, but since these young ladies seldom had any money, the farang eventually paid, one way or another.

Anyway, while I was in Bangkok, Willem had Nang come from her village to his home in Udon Thani in order to have a webcam chat with me. I went to an Internet café and saw on the screen a pretty little girl, age 25, whose husband had died some months before. Husband, eh? Did she have any children? At my age, with a strong desire for peace and quiet, I was unwilling to go through another period of child-rearing. No children, Willem assured me. Nang did not speak English, so Willem's wife acted as translator.

Nang seemed very sweet and appeared to like me during our web chat, so I arranged to fly to Udon to meet her. I checked into my usual hotel, the Grand Royal, and Willem delivered Nang to me, promising to return after we had become better acquainted.

I had purchased an English-Thai dictionary to aid in the communication process. However, Nang and I got off to a great start without any kind of reference book. She was wearing a nicely decorated tee shirt, and to indicate my approval of her taste in clothes I touched the shirt and nodded with a smile. Nang interpreted this as a request and she obliged by quickly removing the shirt, along with everything else she was wearing.

Who needs a dictionary? I thought and of course I did not attempt to correct her misunderstanding. She proved to be an avid sexual partner, anxious to please me and most able to do so. It occurred to me to hope she had learned her skills from her late husband rather than as a bar girl, but by the time we'd indulged in two hours of nonstop activity I didn't much care.

Nang proved to be very affectionate even when we were not having sex and this was like candy to me, especially after Lin, who had accepted my advances as a sort of duty. So when Willem returned I paid him his fee of 30,000 baht (yes, another $1000) and then we all went to a nearby night market to get some necessities for Nang.

The plan was that we would stay in Udon for two days, go to Bangkok to get married and then travel to her village where I would meet her family and spend another week with my new bride.

While we were still at the Grand Royal I received a phone call from a young Thai woman named Tami, a platonic friend who lived in Udon. I invited her to the hotel room to meet Nang. After the girls had chatted for a while – in Thai, of course – Tami turned to me and said, "Do you know that she has a child?"

After I picked myself up off the floor I explored this little detail with Nang, using Tami as translator. Yes, she had a girl, four-and-a-half years old, by her late husband, but no problem. The child would be raised in Thailand jointly by her mother and mother-in-law. I looked deep into Nang's eyes and repeated my mantra that I did not want to raise a child at my age. No problem, she assured me.

In my lawyer's office in Bangkok we went through all this again and got married. I spent the following week with her in her village as planned, then went home.

I'll spare you most of what followed. I hired Jim's girlfriend Banama to act as translator because, for a number of reasons, I no longer trusted Willem. Not long afterward, Banama broke the news that Nang had changed her mind. I was welcome to move to Thailand and live with her there but she was no longer willing to leave her family and come to the USA.

This was a stunning blow, but a few weeks later she changed her mind again. She would live with me in California for six months and if everything was working out okay she would stay – provided I then bought a new house for her parents in Thailand.

A new house! Nang had not asked for a dowry, but now she was more than making up for this oversight.

My main concern was that after the money for the house reached Thailand she would change her mind one last time and join her family in their new residence, with or without me.

I returned to Thailand for further negotiations with her at my lawyer's office. We didn't seem to be getting anywhere. Finally Nang asked, "Do you want a divorce?" Without thinking it over I said yes and that was that. Maybe this was too hasty of me, but there had been other unsettling episodes with her and this became another relationship where my feeling of trust evaporated.

Perhaps I was influenced too strongly by Lin's thievery. More to the point, I also concluded that it had been unrealistic to expect Nang to leave her child behind.

Lani

Shortly after my divorce from Nang I received a show of interest on ThaiLoveLinks from a 40-year-old woman I will call Lani. One of the photos in her profile was an immediate turn-off because it showed her holding a small boy. Nevertheless, I read her essay and learned that she was a teacher in a small city and was indeed the mother of that small boy.

This was a source of regret to me because her essay was spiced with humor and sophistication – very uncommon in the pages of ThaiLoveLinks.

As a courtesy, I replied, pointing out that my own essay emphatically stated *no children*. I had reminded other interested mothers of this in the past. Some of them wished me luck, others did not answer, and I expected one of these reactions from Lani.

Instead, she insisted that the boy was not an issue and in fact he preferred her mother to her and would be quite happy to be raised by his grandmother.

Where had I heard a story like that before? The obvious next step was for me to send a gracious "thanks but no thanks" note. I did nothing of the sort. Instead, I allowed myself to be seduced by some entertaining web chats with her and arranged to meet her during my next trip to Thailand.

One thing led to another and subsequently she became Thai wife Number 3.

I never met Lani's family, not even her son, but I nevertheless turned over to her the usual dowry and – another Thai custom – a significant amount of gold jewelry. After I returned home her financial requests continued unabated, above and beyond the support money I had agreed to send.

The marriage reached the point of no continuance during a web chat when she asked for an extra $1500, which she said she needed in order to bribe officials to approve her transfer to a school closer to her home.

I pointed out – rather reasonably, I thought – that she was still drawing down her teacher's salary in addition to my support money, and I asked for an accounting of her finances.

She replied that if I did not send the $1500 she would reconsider coming to the USA. Hmmm, more *de javu* all over again. She went on to suggest that maybe we should divorce. I interpreted this as an empty threat designed to bring me to my knees but I proceeded to surprise her by replying, "Okay."

I did not do this lightly. Her previous requirements led me to conclude she was not so much a partner as an adversary.

She then demanded an outrageous $180,000 as a settlement for the divorce – possibly in order to bully me into remaining married to her. I countered by giving her a choice of the $1500 bribe money she said she needed, or $0. She took the $1500.

Lani later informed me that she'd become involved with a Brit she'd flirted with behind my back, early in our marriage – confirmation that this was another relationship I'd been foolish to get into, belatedly smart to get out of.

Well, there you have my three Thai marriages – each of which coincidentally lasted seven months – and the subsequent divorces. Also included, at considerable extra cost, were three visa applications, all of which I revoked before they got to the interview stage.

Important! Please don't let these failures that I have described discourage you from seeking an Asian wife. As

I indicated at the beginning of this chapter, my failures were due in large part to a man of advanced age trying to play "Beat the Clock" and beating himself up in the process. I did not allow nearly enough time to get to know any of the three Thai women I impulsively proposed to, and in each case I determinedly ignored warning sirens that were screaming at me to look elsewhere.

Anyway, despite my determined efforts to mess myself up, everything worked out in time. Instead of hiding under a blanket and swearing off Asian wife-hunting, I emulated the Vegas casino loser who changes his luck by changing slot machines. In short, I changed countries. And I hit the jackpot.

That story is told in the next chapter.

18

I FINALLY GET IT RIGHT

After my Thai experiences I switched countries simply by switching from ThaiLoveLinks to FilipinaHeart (now FilipinoCupid). I soon established contact with three girls and was chatting with them on Yahoo Instant Messenger. The first girl seemed nice enough until our third chat, during which she asked me to send her 1500 pesos (about $33), in return for which she promised to "do whatever I want."

Hmm, whatever I want for only $33. There was just one difficulty and I don't think I need to draw you a diagram. There she was in the Philippines and here I was in the USA. Sure, I could wire her the money but she could not wire me whatever I wanted, and even if I were to travel to the Philippines to collect, there was no reason to believe that the offer was genuine. In any case, I was turned off by her request and I told her goodbye.

The second girl gave every evidence of being genuine and we had a few chats, but then I met Fely online and all thoughts of any other girl quickly disappeared. Fely caused me to break one of my rules. Well, breaking my rules had by now become second nature, but this was a cardinal rule.

I fell in love on the Internet. All of this stuff I had been preaching about the ridiculousness of considering oneself to be in love before even meeting the other person went out the window.

Our webcam chats lasted 2 to 3 hours and we had them every night. This went on for three months and it just became a matter of how soon I could come to the Philippines and marry Fely.

There was just one technicality: I was still married to Lani, my third Thai wife. I can see you rolling your eyes and thinking, "Is this guy totally stupid or senile or both?" Yes, that's a reasonable question, but there was an important difference: I had not felt love for any of the three Thai wives – I had felt only desire. Desire alone is not really good enough to sustain a marriage, but to a man of my age who was determined on marrying a much younger woman it seemed at the time to be all I could hope for. In hindsight, it was wrong to compromise. I should have held out for love.

As I write this, Fely and I have been married for three terrific years. The first of those years was spent going through the tortuous immigration process, which I will describe in the next chapter.

Advice from Fely

Here's Fely, with a Filipina's point of view:

"I want to give you some advice about chatting with women that are on Internet sites. Of course, most singles who are looking for real love really want a perfect match. Make sure that you are:

"**Sincere:** Don't be in a relationship with somebody else. You have to be open with her. If you have a problem with her, let her know what bothers you and remind her if she does it again next time.

"Honest: both of you have to be honest with each other and not over-protective because sometimes the woman doesn't like that. It's normal to be jealous but not too much and don't accuse her about something without proof. Most important, you don't have to chat with other women because that is why some relationships do not work.

"Considerate: Most single girls don't have their own computer, so they have to go to an Internet café. So if the woman says that she cannot chat tomorrow or the next day because of a financial problem, think about sending her some money for the Internet chats, but I warn you, do not send a big amount of money because you do not know her in person.

"It is best to find a young Asian fiancée or wife because we don't care about the age gap and we are the best wife to take care of you, as long as you are nice, sincere, and serious, and accept us even if we come from a poor family. We don't want too much drinking.

"When you visit her in person look at her attitude, her history, family, and friends. If she's very kind and you're sure that she's the one, you can propose to her. But do not marry her till you know her better, because some women want you for your money only. Good luck!"

19

OUR MARRIAGE VISA

Now that I'd finally found the right one, I had to get her home. I was really worried about my prospects, because I had already applied for two fiancée visas and three CR1 spousal visas. All of this was on file at the State Department and I would have to include the whole sorry history in the new application. The one thing going for me was the fact that I had canceled the visa applications for my three Thai wives when I found them unsuitable, which I hoped would be convincing evidence that I was not a total idiot and I wasn't playing games with the immigration service. Time would tell.

I'll take you through the actual experiences Fely and I had with the officials of our respective countries. The beginning of the story is a lesson on how the bureaucrats can punish you if there is a minor discrepancy in your application.

It all began routinely. Three weeks after my paralegal Ray Bacon filed our paperwork, I received a receipt notice, which included a WAC number that would be Fely's ID number throughout the process. The next notice I got was a bombshell. It was called a Request for Evidence (RFE) and it took the form of a three-and-a-half-page document specifying additional evidence that was now required.

The notice was triggered by an unintentional omission on Ray's part. He had sent proof of my three Thai divorces in the form of certified translations from the Thai language into English. This did not satisfy the authorities. They also wanted the original documents that were in the Thai language.

Fair enough, and one might think they would be satisfied if I forwarded those three papers, but now they piled on with this "request" for many additional documents that I had never been asked for in any of my applications. I was warned that failure to provide these documents might result in the denial of my application. Bear in mind, this evidence was supposedly requested as further proof that my marriage to Fely was sincere and legitimate, or, as they put it, *bona fide*.

Okay, let's examine the kind of evidence the USCIS was requesting. I won't include all of it – that would be a whole chapter in itself – just a few highlights to give you an idea of the government's thinking.

I was asked if all of Fely's siblings attended our wedding. If not, I was to submit a notarized statement from each absent sibling giving the reason why he or she did not attend. To this day, it is unclear to me how the absence of a brother or sister would undermine the validity of our marriage, especially as my original application had included photos of the wedding and the reception, plus, of course, the certificate of marriage. However, I dutifully obtained handwritten statements by Fely's brother and one of her sisters explaining why they had been unable to attend the wedding.

In retrospect, I needn't have gone to all that trouble, as the Feds had no way of knowing who had, or had not, been at our wedding, but at the time I was intimidated by these official demands.

Another request was for the birth certificates of my parents – again, something that had never previously been sought. My parents had died more than 50 years ago and I somehow didn't have their birth certificates.

An additional test of the validity of our marriage was a request for the receipt for our wedding ring. Unfortunately, I had thrown away the receipt, not having been savvy enough to realize that someday a government agency would want to review this important piece of evidence.

There was more, lots more, and it took me a week to dig up and photocopy the documents that I could lay my hands on. The package I sent contained 120 pages of material plus 20 more photos of Fely and me together.

All of these "make work" requests were examples of senseless and possibly malicious harassment by an anonymous (of course!) employee – requests that had no bearing on whether or not our marriage was *bona fide*.

After all that garbage was sent off, I finally received a notice that my application had been accepted and was being forwarded to the US Embassy in Manila.

Fely's Part

Subsequently, Fely received a notice from the embassy that she had an appointment for an interview on March 4, 2011. Prior to that date she would have to get a police report showing that she did not have a criminal record, and a medical examination conducted at St. Luke's Medical Extension near the embassy.

Of course, she also had to have her passport, and obtaining that was another example of bureaucracy gone rampant – this time on the part of the Philippine government. In the Philippines, you can't simply apply for a passport as we do here. As a Philippine national, you must first apply for a certificate that allows you to apply for a passport! In the chapter titled "Getting Her Here," I describe this process.

So Fely had to make an overnight trip to a government office in Cebu for yet another counseling session, which took half a day. With the certificate in hand, she went back to a government office in Tacloban, where she was able to apply for the passport.

I wanted to be with Fely for both her medical exam and the interview, so I purchased a round-trip flight to Manila and a ticket for Fely to fly back with me on March 18, two weeks after her interview. (Embassy processing times for visas are 7-10 days.)

But then the embassy changed her appointment from March 4 to Feb. 23. This threw the proverbial monkey wrench into our travel plans. There wasn't enough time for me to join Fely for her medical exam and the best I could do was to arrange for her to fly to Manila and stay at a hotel prior to the exam. I would arrive the day before her interview.

Fely consulted with Lucia, Ray Bacon's associate in Manila. Lucia's advice was as follows:

"Dress well for the interview. Smile and have a confident attitude. Don't lie about anything. Be prepared for questions about the age difference between you and your husband as well as sexual relations with your husband and, if you had them, with other men. Know the dates of your husband's visits and of your honeymoon and other travels. Be prepared to show a record of all financial help from your husband."

Lucia's advice was pretty well on target, as you'll see when I describe the interview shortly. But first …

The Medical Exam

Here, in Fely's own words, is her experience with the medical exam:

"When I received the notice of my interview at the US Embassy in Manila, I had to go first to St. Luke's for a medical exam. Actually, there are two St. Luke's and the one to use is St. Luke's Medical Extension on Bocobo Street, Ermita, right near the embassy.

"I called Lucia, the person who is helping me with my application, and asked her if I need an appointment for the medical. She said no, just come to Manila and bring my interview notice plus four 1x1-inch ID pictures, birth certificate, marriage contract, and passport.

"Before you can go inside St. Luke's, the guard will want to see your papers and then when you are inside you have to fill out a form and get a number and when your number is called you get on line and give them your papers. Then you pay the medical fee of 9,814.10 pesos (US $213).

"When I saw the doctor I told her that I have my menstruation, so she told me I would have to come back after my period was over. Meanwhile, I was able to get part of the medical exam, where they got a urine and blood sample and then the chest x-ray where I had to take my top and bra off in front of 15 or 20 people.

"Then I had the immunization interview where a doctor asked about all kinds of diseases I might have had and they gave me three vaccinations. After that they told me to come back again when my period was over.

"When I came back I went to a small room where the doctor told me to take off all my clothes and then she examined all my parts including my private parts. When the examination was finished I had to leave my passport because it will be delivered with the results of the exam to the US Embassy in time for the interview. They gave me a CD of my x-ray which I was told to bring to the US and hand over to the immigration officers at my port of entry with a copy of my vaccination record.

"I was walking out of the clinic on cloud nine. Such a relief! By that time my husband arrived to be with me for my interview at the embassy. I'm so happy!"

The Interview

We were instructed to arrive at the US Embassy at 6:30 AM. When we showed up, there were already about 100 people assembled on benches outside of the building. We got inside after a wait of about an hour. We were directed to a large room in which maybe 200 people were seated.

When Fely's name was eventually called she went to a counter where she received a pre-interview screening by a Filipina. During the screening, Fely was asked to produce her documents and answer such questions as her date of birth, my date of birth, and a few other details to prove that she was familiar with the man she was married to.

After that was successfully concluded, we waited some more and then finally were summoned to an interview room. This was a small room in which we were seated across a counter facing our interviewer. He greeted us with a look of sheer displeasure and it was hard to tell whether his attitude was general for all interviewees or specific to us. I had much trepidation regarding what I considered to be two strikes against me. One was the number of my previous marriages, and the other was the age difference between us of 60-plus years.

After a few perfunctory questions the official asked me to wait outside. He then asked Fely the following questions: When did we first communicate? When was our first meeting? Then the questions got personal and in my view the one that crossed the line was a question about whether Fely had given me her body on our first night together. I cannot see what bearing this has on whether or not a visa should be issued to her, but here again, he had the power and he was free to use it and abuse it.

Other questions dealt with where we spent our honeymoon, whether I sent her money, and if she was sure of her relationship with me.

He then suggested to Fely that she had chosen an old man so she could get to the USA and then leave him and find someone younger. Fely replied that she felt that an older man has more wisdom and maturity and that is why she liked me. She also added that I was nice and sincere. Throughout all of this, the interviewer remained stern. At one point, even though her English is good, Fely had some difficulty understanding some of the questions and a Filipina was brought in to act as translator.

After her questioning, Fely was sent outside and I was called in. The interviewer asked me pretty much the same questions that he had asked Fely except that he did not discuss the sexual matters, perhaps thinking that I, as a US citizen, might ask him what business that was of his.

He then asked me about my Thai divorces. As there is no divorce in the Philippines, he seemed interested in the legal process of divorce in Thailand. I gave him a rather humorous explanation and soon he was relaxed and laughing. The ice had been broken.

There followed a question about my relationship with Fely and this time there was no humor in my response. I became genuinely emotional and tears filled my eyes when I told him how much I appreciated and loved her and I assured him, with the sincerity that I feel to this day – and will always feel – that Fely and I will remain married forever. His response came quickly and tersely. "All right, your visa is granted. Go to the next window."

I thanked him warmly, but he had reverted back to the cold bureaucrat. I didn't care. I was out of there. I gave Fely the wonderful news and we went to the next window.

There we were told that her visa and other documents would be delivered by courier to the address on her application. I replied that we had moved out and were living in a hotel in Manila and therefore we would like to pick up the papers when they were ready. The official said we could obtain the papers from the courier service in Manila.

Now we were both on cloud nine.

It Still Wasn't Over!

The bureaucracy wasn't done with us yet. The final complication came when we arrived at LAX – home free, we thought, but not quite. When our turn came to go to the immigration desk, my passport was stamped and we were sent to another section that handled first-time arrivals. After a wait of about an hour, Fely was summoned by an official and asked for the sealed packet of papers from the embassy. I was watching from my seat several rows back when I saw Fely frantically signaling me to join her.

The immigration officer told me that three important papers were missing from the envelope. I was stunned to learn that they were the original Thai divorce documents that had caused the National Visa Center in New Hampshire to send me that request for evidence.

It appeared that after all the fuss they had made about the missing divorce papers, which I had subsequently sent to them, they did not include those very documents with the rest of Fely's paperwork!

Trying to keep my cool, I told all this to the immigration officer, but he was looking at us as if this were somehow our fault, even though we had simply handed him a sealed package from the embassy. I had visions – practically hallucinations – of Fely being deported back to the Philippines.

Suddenly I remembered that I had photocopies of the papers with me. I gave these to the officer and even though they were not strictly legal because they were not in the sealed package, he apparently decided that this was the best way to resolve the situation and accepted my copies. Much relieved, we were finally out of the airport and truly home free.

20

CRITICISMS OF AN OLD MAN WITH A YOUNG WIFE

In this book I think I was pretty merciless about my foolishness in the three "serial" Thai marriages I indulged in. Now I am going to defend myself against the criticism that is often levied against a man who marries a woman of a much younger age.

Actually, all of the busybody complaints about our marriage thus far have been directed at Fely from some of her distant relatives and neighbors in the Philippines.

The gist of their snide remarks is that Fely married me solely in order to get to the United States and then leave me for a more suitable younger man. Why else would a woman in her 20s marry a man in his 80s?

In addition to being obnoxiously rude by voicing these comments, especially to Fely's face, these people – whose spite was likely motivated by their envy of someone who no longer shared their poor standard of living – were totally wrong in their assumptions. Fely and I are living an extremely happy life together, day and night, and the age difference simply doesn't enter into our marriage.

Admittedly, this is aided by the fact that I have been fortunate enough to retain most of the energy and zest for life I had as a much younger man. At the age of 75 I stopped flying airplanes and took up scuba diving instead. I continue my main vocation as a professional writer and my part-time work as an actor, occasionally appearing in TV commercials. I also do public speaking and every so often a singing gig. And as some previous chapters in this book have indicated, my libido is right up there.

Most important, Fely and I truly love and respect each other, and underneath our frequent teasing is a strong foundation of caring and concern for each other's needs. I could not ask for a better marriage regardless of our respective ages.

But, some might argue, am I not being self-indulgent, considering that age will inevitably take its toll, leaving my wife to cope with a husband as he goes downhill physically and/or mentally? Yes, one could say that. No man knows how his life will end, but I have plans to make that end swift and painless. Furthermore, I will leave Fely well provided for and very likely she will still be a young woman, a US citizen, and in a good position to start a new chapter in her life.

I hope that all men, regardless of age differences, will meet a similar standard – and while I have many things to apologize for, marrying a much younger woman is not one of them.

21

CONCLUSION

I trust you've found in these pages a lot of useful information, fleshed out by examples of my own experiences, to help you in your quest for the Asian wife of your dreams. Or, if marriage is not really your goal, to point the way to fun-filled escapades with charming women overseas.

I've made some mistakes along the way and I think I've described them in sufficiently embarrassing detail. You won't make those particular errors, I'm sure.

And despite all of my foolhardiness, I've had some glorious adventures. In my 70s and 80s, when many of my contemporaries were playing shuffleboard in Florida, I was frolicking with a satisfying number of attractive young women on the beach and in the bed.

You can do likewise, and I'm pretty certain you're a lot younger than I am. Just pay close attention to warning signals and avoid the kind of traps I recklessly plunged into. Also, I hope you'll play fair with the women you meet and not make promises you have no intention of keeping.

If you're serious about finding a sweet Asian wife, I'm confident that you can do it. There are so many of them out there, looking eagerly for a man they can love – a man from a country like ours, who can offer them a much better life than they'll ever get at home.

I did it. I persevered through some setbacks and I am rewarded every day by the companionship of my darling, affectionate, funny, always interesting wife Fely.

Both of us had to jump through a lot of hoops to satisfy the officials in our respective governments. It was worth it because she is here now and the concerns are all behind us.

Well, mostly behind us, because we have applied to renew her green card – which could result in another interview with more intrusive questions – but soon after that she will qualify to become an American citizen, free from the immigration bureaucracy.

As I write this, there is much talk about immigration reform – that is, reforming the way illegal immigrants are handled. That's fine, but there also needs to be considerable reform of the way people who are playing by the rules are treated – legal immigrants and their sponsors who are citizens of the country our government is supposed to be serving in a humane way.

I invite you to see updates and discussions on the various subjects covered in this book by visiting my blog at http://Men4AsianWomen.com.

With best wishes,

Keith Connes

APPENDIX

This Appendix contains a listing of resources that provide additional information on many of the subjects I've covered. Some of the resources have already been mentioned elsewhere in this book, but I'm assembling them in one place for your convenience. I have personally read the books and visited the websites I've listed. Obviously, you can find many additional resources by searching the Web.

Relevant Websites

ThaiLoveLinks.com, where I met many interesting Thai women. The site is user-friendly and offers several levels of membership. The Gold membership met my needs very nicely.

FilipinoCupid.com, (formerly FilipinaHeart). This is under the same ownership as ThaiLoveLinks and operates in the same way. As I was fortunate enough to meet my lovely Filipina wife Fely very quickly, I was not an active member for long.

Christian-Filipina.com. Despite its name, membership is open to people of non-Christian religions or even no religion at all. Regardless, many of the women's profiles mention religion as being an important part of their lives. As a registered male member I got my heart started each day, when I automatically received an email with photos and profiles of a dozen ladies. Their blog provides many tips on negotiating the Philippine singles scene.

Thailandguru.com – not a matchmaking website – is directed primarily to expats and provides a host of information on housing, visas, and working abroad.

StickmanBangkok.com is an exhaustively thorough series of essays (the author claims that the opening page is just under 100,000 words and I believe him!) on an expat's life in Thailand, particularly Bangkok. His lengthy commentary on working conditions for a Westerner in a Thai society are very instructive for an American who is considering employment in Thailand.

Relevant Books

A Man's Guide to Life and Love in the Philippines by Larry Elterman. This book is chock-full of information. A lot of it is from the point of view of an expat because that's what the author is. One of his chapters, titled *The Best Places for Expats to Live*, describes about a dozen cities an American might consider if he plans to move to the Philippines. There is little or no mention of dealing with the tortuous process of bringing a foreign wife or fiancée to the USA. Regardless of where you plan to live, I highly recommend Larry's book as a complementary resource to the book you are now reading. (But if you are a grammatical purist, prepare to grin and bear it.)

Culture Shock! A Survival Guide to Customs and Etiquette (in the) Philippines by Alfredo and Grace Roces. This is one of a series of *Culture Shock!* guidebooks covering such additional countries as China, India, Costa Rica, and Chile (but not Thailand). I have read only the Philippines version, which, like Elterman's book described above, is heavily oriented to expat life, with considerable information on such subjects as Philippine culture, food, health care, and transportation. The authors have a sophisticated literary style, enhanced by cartoons and photographs. In other words, it's a "good read" but don't expect strategies on finding the girl of your dreams.

Thailand Fever by Chris Pirazzi and Vitida Vasant. This is a relationship guide, designed to help a mixed couple – Western male and Thai female – build mutual trust through a greater understanding of each other's culture and expectations. A unique and useful feature of this book is its bi-lingual format – that is, the text is in English on each left-hand page and the corresponding text is in Thai on the opposing right-hand page. This enables the couple to read the book together in linguistic harmony.

Traditional Guidebooks

There are zillions of guidebooks available. What I refer to as the "traditional" guidebooks are those that give an overview of a particular country, with introductory sections on major tourist attractions, currency, climate, and transportation, followed by details about each location's places of interest, accommodations, and restaurants.

In my travels I used the Rough Guide and Footprint guide to Thailand and the Lonely Planet guide to the Philippines. They were all good, but no single book can tell you all you need to know about a country. So you can either do a lot of research via the Internet, public library, well-travelled friends, and a travel agent who's actually spent some time there – or simply charge ahead with a guidebook or two and learn the rest by adventure.

Networking Groups

MAG-ANAK@yahoogroups.com. This is a private mailing list for discussion of Filipino/Non-Filipino relationships. Members advise each other on cultural adjustments, immigration and other legal matters, and additional issues regarding these bi-cultural relationships. Many of the members are American expats living in the Philippines with their Filipino wives. I have been a member for several years and have exchanged some useful information and I have also seen some postings that are heavily biased and inaccurate – but those statements are usually corrected by other members.

ExpatFocus.com provides considerable information to people who have relocated to various countries, including Thailand and the Philippines. Among other features on their website are detailed comments from expats concerning the joys and downsides of the moves they have made.

InterNations.org is another organization catering to expats who have relocated to virtually any country. Once you join you will receive frequent email invitations to events in your area. Their website offers various types of information and a forum.

And My Blog

Again, a reminder to visit my blog at http://Men4AsianWomen.com to view updated information and to join in on whatever discussions arouse your interest.

INDEX

About the Author

Keith Connes spent the first half of his life in New York City and its environs and began his career writing and producing radio and TV commercials. He took up private flying as a hobby and that led him into becoming an aviation writer and editor. During the ensuing years he published more than 150 aviation articles and two aviation books, the latter in seven editions. At age 75 he stopped flying and took up scuba diving. However, his most interesting pursuit has been that of younger women, as related in this book. To pass the time on long flights to Thailand and the Philippines he began writing short stories, some of which are now available as eBooks on Kindle and Nook.

He lives with his wife Fely in southern California.

www.ingramcontent.com/pod-product-compliance
Lightning Source LLC
Chambersburg PA
CBHW052104090426
42741CB00009B/1672